SECRET
JOHANNESBURG
AN UNUSUAL GUIDE

C. L. Bell and Lisa Johnston

JONGLEZ PUBLISHING

travel guides

NOTE FROM THE AUTHORS

Lisa Johnston is a writer and photographer who was born and grew up in Johannesburg. She has worked variously as a travel, design and art journalist and is drawn to the unique creative pulse of the city and its people. In her early adult years, Johnston tried on various occasions to leave Johannesburg for a quieter life, both locally and abroad, but Joburg's combination of grit, green and glamour kept calling her back. She has lived the past 15 years in Johannesburg and has given up her quest for a country life, focusing instead on growing an urban farm in her small garden not far from the city.

C. L. Bell grew up on Johannesburg's East Rand, and fell in love with the city at the age of 5, when she first caught a train downtown. A journalist and investigative researcher, she has a masters degree in philosophy from Birkbeck College in London and writes the blog UnpopularEssays.com. She loves how Joburg is at the epicentre of social, political and cultural change. Bell is part of the team that runs Consciousness Café, a pop-up dialogue café that brings South Africans together in galleries, community centres and gardens around the city to have uncomfortable conversations about how the politics of the past still overshadow the present and to encourage deep democracy – where every voice is heard and valued.

NOTE FROM THE EDITOR

We have taken great pleasure in drawing up *Secret Johannesburg* and hope that through its guidance you will, like us, continue to discover unusual, hidden or little-known aspects of the city.
Descriptions of certain places are accompanied by thematic sections highlighting historical details or anecdotes as an aid to understanding the city in all its complexity.
Secret Johannesburg also draws attention to the multitude of details found in places that we may pass every day without noticing. These are an invitation to look more closely at the urban landscape and, more generally, a means of seeing our own city with the curiosity and attention that we often display while travelling elsewhere ...

Comments on this guidebook and its contents, as well as information on places we may not have mentioned, are more than welcome and will enrich future editions.

Don't hesitate to contact us:
- Jonglez Publishing, 25 rue du Maréchal Foch, 78000 Versailles, France
- E-mail : info@jonglezpublishing.com

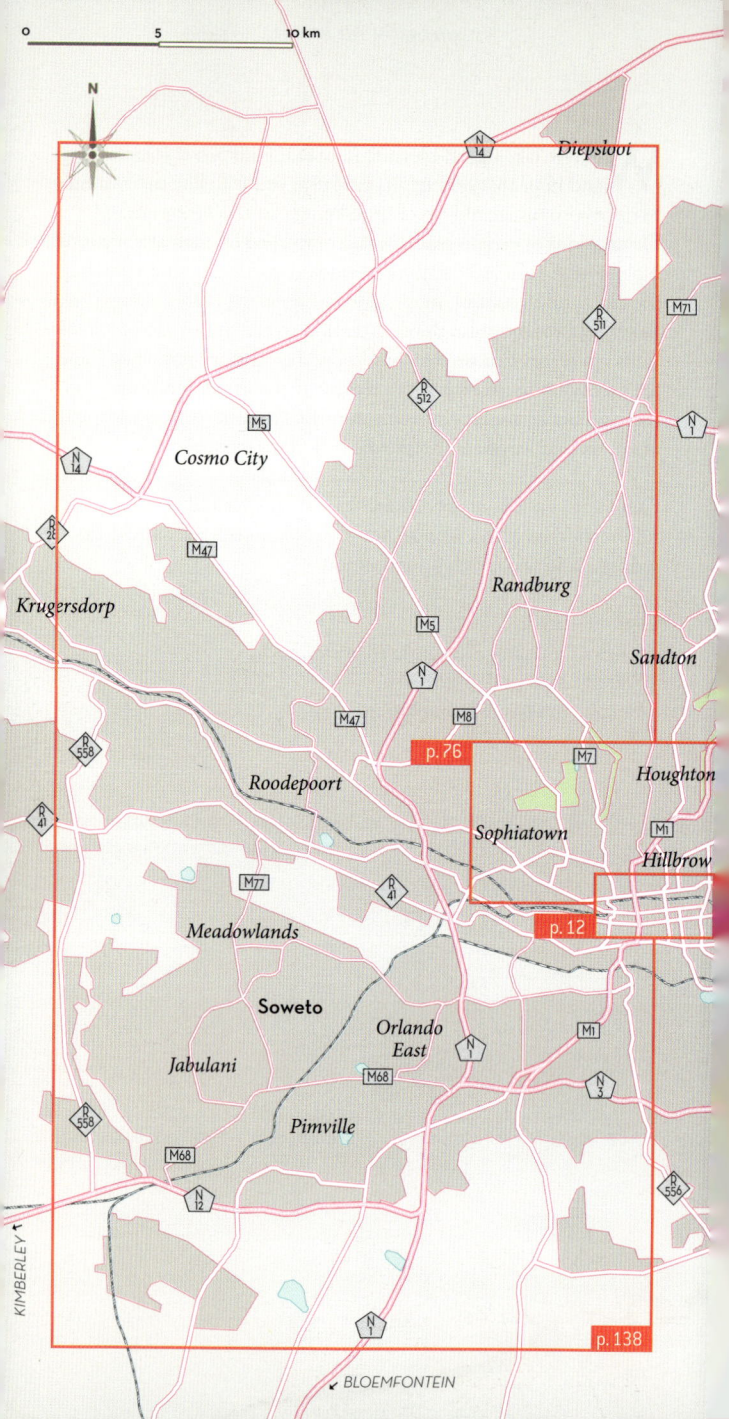

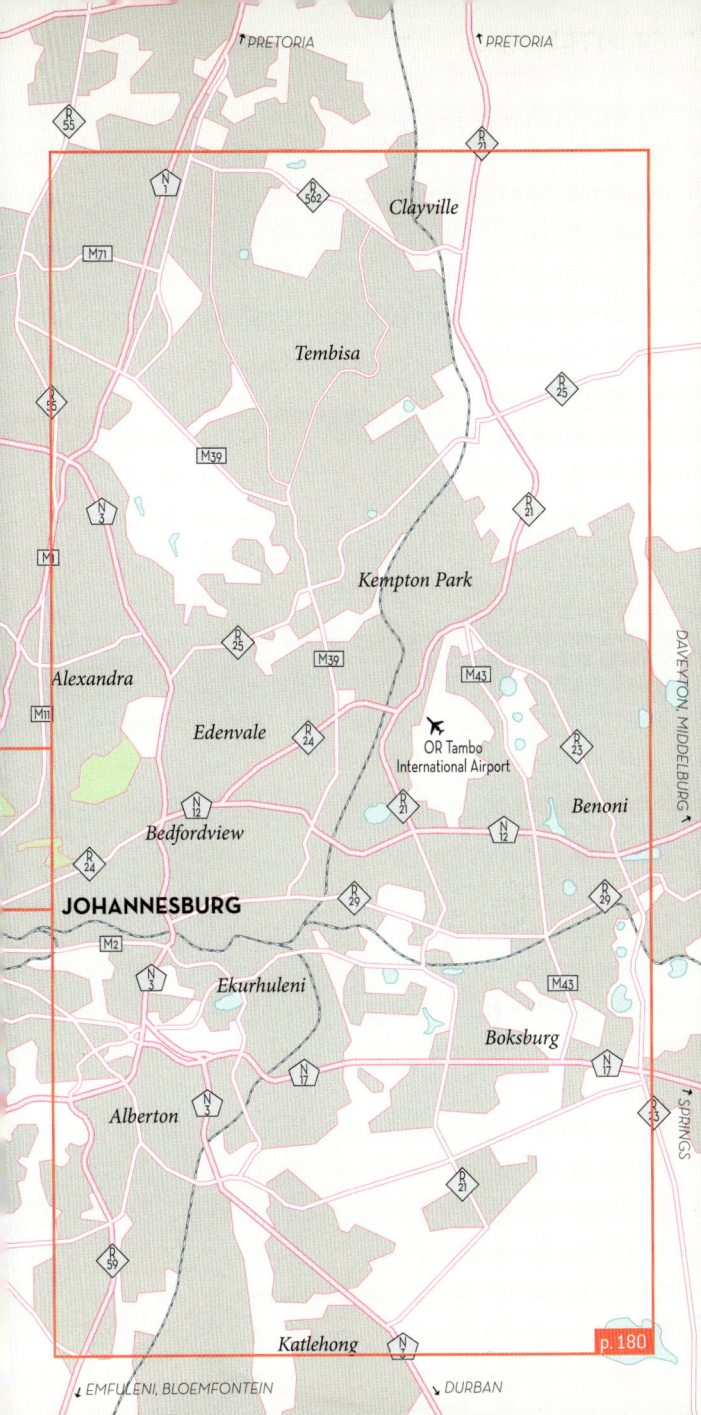

CONTENTS

Downtown Joburg

THE STREET ART OF HANNELIE COETZEE	14
LUSCIOUS LIPS GRAFFITI	16
THE BERNBERG DRESSES	18
DIAZ CROSS	20
OLD PROTEST TREASURES	22
A COLLECTION OF 16TH, 17TH AND 18TH CENTURY HARPSICHORDS	24
KERK STREET MOSQUE	26
OLD JOHANNESBURG STOCK EXCHANGE TRADING FLOOR	28
ANGLO AMERICAN DOORS	30
MASTERPIECES IN THE MAGISTRATE'S COURT	32
THE STRANGE STACKS	34
ROCK ART OF THE VOLK	36
THE LIGHTHOUSE IN THE SKY	38
ROCKFACE	40
CORNER HOUSE'S CUPOLA	42
CUTHBERT'S CUPOLA	44
CECILY SASH MOSAIC IN LITTLE ETHIOPIA	46
THE SPACESHIP MAST	48
TRANSNET'S MYSTERY ARCHIVE	50
LARRY SCULLY MURALS	52
WINDYBROW	54
POETRY STEPS	56
MOTHER THERESA'S BLESSING	58
THE OLD VICTORIAN HOTHOUSE	60
TWIST STREET BENCH	62
THE GREEN OFFICE	64
POST OFFICE MURALS	66
ADOLF HITLER'S TYPEWRITER	68
ST. MARY'S THE LESS CHURCH	70
SALISBURY HOUSE	72
VESTIGES OF A TRAM STATION	74

Sophiatown, The Parks, Houghton

BALDINELLI'S MOSAIC OF JESUS	78
SONS OF ENGLAND CROSS	80
HOUGHTON WATERFALL	82
MINIATURE RAILWAY OF OBSERVATORY	84
MAGNETIC ROCKS OF OBS	86
YUKON'S MISSING WINDOWS	88
YEOVILLE'S FESTIVAL BELLS	90
HERMAN CHARLES BOSMAN IN JOHANNESBURG	92
BAMBANANI URBAN GARDEN	94
TROYEVILLE'S "BEDTIME STORY"	96
SCULPTURES IN AN OVERGROWN LOT	98
HIGHLANDS ROAD SCOTTISH VESTIGES	100
DAVID WEBSTER HOUSE	102
BYZANTINE PLUMBER'S YARD	104
MR. TRILETY'S NOSE SHAPER	106
THE SPRINGBOK OF THE REGIMENTAL HQ OF THE TRANSVAAL SCOTTISH	108
VILLA ARCADIA	110
THE MESSERSCHMITT 262 JET NIGHT FIGHTER	112
HYDE PARK SHOPPING CENTRE ART COLLECTION	114
MELVILLE WATERFALL	116
HISTORIC FRENCH PRESS IN "THE ATELIER"	118
LAM RIM TIBETAN BUDDHIST CENTRE	120
FIETAS MUSEUM	122
CHAMPION TREES	124
CHURCH OF ST. NICHOLAS OF JAPAN	126
LINDFIELD VICTORIAN HOUSE MUSEUM	128
THE PARANOID TREE	130
GAUTENG'S ARTESIAN SPRING	132
TREVOR HUDDLESTON'S CENOTAPH	134
SOPHIATOWN'S HERITAGE TREE	136

CONTENTS

Greater Joburg: Soweto, North and West

EDOARDO'S VILLA	140
GARDEN OF ST. CHRISTOPHER	142
EDOARDO VILLA'S "CONFRONTATION" SCULPTURE	144
MANDELA'S MISSING PISTOL	146
IRON AGE FURNACES BURIED IN A PARK	148
JFK MEMORIAL	150
ROBERT "SPILLER" VAN TONDER GRAVE	152
MOGALE'S GATE BIODIVERSITY CENTRE	154
NAMELESS GRAVES OF THE BURGERSHOOP CEMETERY	156
MTN ART COLLECTION	158
LILIAN NGOYI MEMORIAL	160
THE CRADLE OF SOWETO	162
ORLANDO PIRATES PAINTING	164
BIRD WATCHING IN SOWETO	166
CREDO MUTWA VILLAGE	168
ANTI-XENOPHOBIA SCULPTURES	170
ENOCH SONTONGA HILL	172
SS MENDI MEMORIAL	174
THE SHARPEVILLE HUMAN RIGHTS PRECINCT	176

Greater Joburg: Alex and East

RASTA VILLAGE	180
IKASI GYM PAINTINGS	182
MOVING FEAST	184
WHERE GANDHI MEDITATED	186
THE LINKSFIELD HOME OF L. RON HUBBARD	188
SCHOENSTATT SHRINE	190
A SCENIC FLIGHT IN A DC3	192
GET MARRIED IN A BOEING 747	194
THE FLAMINGOS OF BENONI	196
SNOWBOARDING ON KLEINFONTEIN MINE DUMP	198
REDAN ROCK ENGRAVINGS	200
THE WHISKY TRAIN	202
COSMOS FLOWER PATHWAYS	204

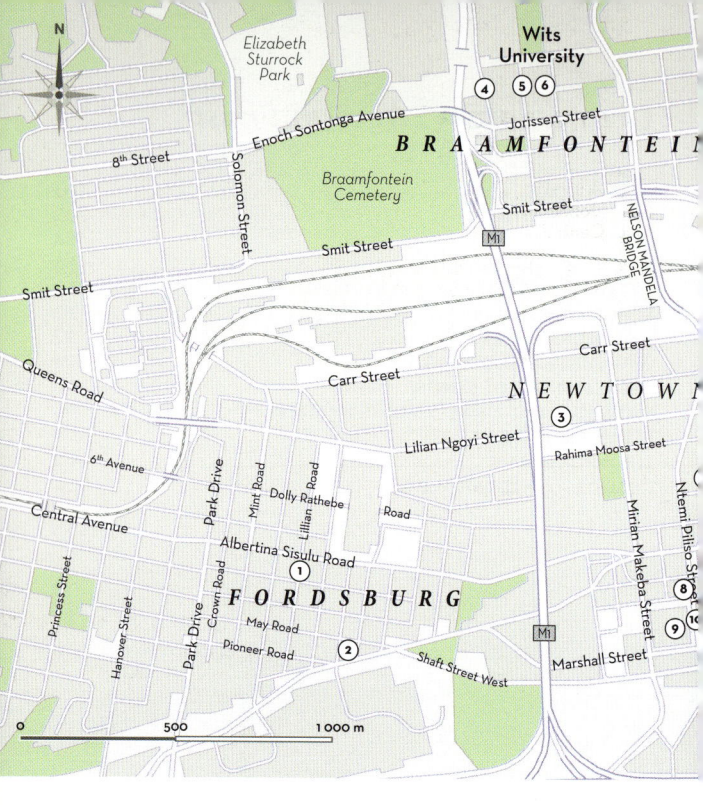

Downtown Joburg

①	THE STREET ART OF HANNELIE COETZEE	14
②	LUSCIOUS LIPS GRAFFITI	16
③	THE BERNBERG DRESSES	18
④	DIAZ CROSS	20
⑤	OLD PROTEST TREASURES	22
⑥	A COLLECTION OF 16TH, 17TH AND 18TH CENTURY HARPSICHORDS	24
⑦	KERK STREET MOSQUE	26
⑧	OLD JOHANNESBURG STOCK EXCHANGE TRADING FLOOR	28
⑨	ANGLO AMERICAN DOORS	30
⑩	MASTERPIECES IN THE MAGISTRATE'S COURT	32
⑪	THE STRANGE STACKS	34
⑫	ROCK ART OF THE VOLK	36
⑬	THE LIGHTHOUSE IN THE SKY	38
⑭	ROCKFACE	40
⑮	CORNER HOUSE'S CUPOLA	42
⑯	CUTHBERT'S CUPOLA	44
⑰	CECILY SASH MOSAIC IN LITTLE ETHIOPIA	46

⑱	THE SPACESHIP MAST	48
⑲	TRANSNET'S MYSTERY ARCHIVE	50
⑳	LARRY SCULLY MURALS	52
㉑	WINDYBROW	54
㉒	POETRY STEPS	56
㉓	MOTHER THERESA'S BLESSING	58
㉔	THE OLD VICTORIAN HOTHOUSE	60
㉕	TWIST STREET BENCH	62
㉖	THE GREEN OFFICE	64
㉗	POST OFFICE MURALS	66
㉘	ADOLF HITLER'S TYPEWRITER	68
㉙	ST. MARY'S THE LESS CHURCH	70
㉚	SALISBURY HOUSE	72
㉛	VESTIGES OF A TRAM STATION	74

THE STREET ART OF HANNELIE COETZEE

Confronting work that confronts

Lilian Street / Jan Smuts Avenue / JAG car park
Open: All day, every day

Tucked away at ankle height, between two galleries on the Rosebank art strip, is a mosaic of a baby Doberman lifting its leg, a trickle of yellow mosaic pee spilling onto the pavement.

"It's obvious that it's about making your mark," says artist Hannelie Coetzee who installed the mosaic illegally in 2010.

At the time, Coetzee, an Afrikaans woman, was exploring her own hurt and anger in the post-apartheid space.

"I was trying to settle into my own skin in this country," she says. "I felt if I could immerse myself in my own history and understand it, I would be able to operate better in this changed world."

Another soul-searching piece is a black and white mosaic of her *Ouma Grootjie* (great grandmother – see below), on the sidewall of a Pakistani food store on Lilian Street in Fordsburg, installed with the permission of the building's Muslim owners.

"I went to sites where my family had once been, so I could question those places," explains Coetzee, "I have been criticized for perpetuating colonisation, for putting Afrikaner histories up, but it was a phase. As an artist I had to process that stuff. I wanted to know my real history. Not just *maanskyn en rosé* (moonshine and roses)."

Her third hidden piece, covered with bird droppings, is in the car park of the Johannesburg Art Gallery: a small beehive house modelled on the Mpeti huts used by Basutho cattle herders, made from sandstone slabs engraved with names. The slabs had initially been made for the war hero memorial wall at Freedom Park. They were rejected and Coetzee stumbled upon them by chance as they were destined for landfill.

"They wouldn't release the new list of heroes. They knew I was onto something," says Coetzee, who suspects the names are of soldiers killed in the Angolan border war in the last days of apartheid. She built the house to be a place for introspection. "I used to come here to get a sense of the city's noises." Inside, a hat and a few coins suggest it is still an urban retreat.

So poor, they would queue to get free blood from the slaughterhouse

Like thousands of others, Coetzee's Ouma Grootjie had arrived in the city destitute after the defeat by the British in the South African War. Living as bywoners (squatters) in a Fordsburg backyard, the family were so poor, they would queue to get free blood from the slaughterhouse to mix with biscuit to make blood rusks, their only source of protein.

LUSCIOUS LIPS GRAFFITI

②

White Jewish boys are the ones with the money to buy paint

Various streets
Marshalltown, Fordsburg, Newtown

Drive or walk around inner city Jo'burg and every so often you'll spot a pair of luscious lips spray painted on a wall. While other graffiti comes and goes, painted over by artists in competing crews, these lips remain out of homage and respect to their artist, Pastelheart, who died in 2015.

Speaking in 2014, to the *Mail & Guardian*, Pastelheart said, "I am willing to give [these lips] to the public unconditionally, as long as the critics do not 'bite' my style. I focus on being carefree towards the negativity of the world. Just make art. This way you won't harm those around you."

Nowadays, the warehouses and rundown buildings of Fordsburg and Marshalltown are thick with lurid tags and paste-ups. But it wasn't always this way. The city in the late 1980s was no place for graffiti: the apartheid state valued order over self-expression.

At the time, hip-hop culture was bubbling up at the opposite end of the country. In an underground club in Cape Town, Prophets of Da City (POC) were emerging as the crew to watch. Channelling the ideas of Steve Biko and Abdullah Ibrahim, POC became famous for their social commentary, producing songs that squared up to the changing and volatile South African landscape.

When, in 1993, the Independent Electoral Commission hired POC to create a national voter campaign, hip-hop cultured shifted from underground to centre stage, unintentionally sanctioning spray cans in downtown Jo'burg.

So while the establishment still regards graffiti as vandalism, to the spraycan artists it is a language of secret nods, winks and codes among those who choose the street as their canvas.

"If you don't understand it, then it's not for you, so f**k you," says graffiti artist Sandile who grew up in inner city Jo'burg. "We're not trying to get people to know what's going on, 'cos it's illegal."

Another thing that is often misunderstood is the identity of these artists. While graffiti is often presumed to be the preserve of black culture, in downtown Jo'burg, the most prolific artists are the white Jewish boys.

"They are the ones with the money to buy paint," says Sandile with a shrug.

Financial constraints also plagued Pastelheart, but he was philosophical. To the *Mail & Guardian* he said, "I believe that I have to discontinue all thoughts that encourage giving up. You have to make art when you have nothing that shows that you have the right motives."

THE BERNBERG DRESSES

The ultimate walk-in cupboard

Museum Africa
Lilian Ngoyi Street
Open: By appointment with fashion curator Pholoso More
Tel: 071-499-4991

"The public has no idea what we have in here," says Pholoso More, the fashion curator of Museum Africa, unlocking the double doors and switching off the alarm system that protects Africa's biggest collection of Edwardian and Victorian gowns and accessories.

This vast collection of dresses, suspended from the ceiling like beautifully dressed ghosts, once belonged to Jewish sisters Anna and Theresa Bernberg, who had been avid collectors (and wearers) of period fashion.

"They were flamboyant in their tastes. There is even a purple wedding dress," says More, explaining that the sisters bought the dresses to wear, and were often seen in the first half of the last century flouncing around Jo'burg in eccentric outfits.

Two of the most valuable garments are a rare Voortrekker dress, and an outfit worn by Princess Anne, granddaughter of Queen Victoria, in 1919.

When the sisters died in the mid-1960s, they bequeathed their frocks and their Forest Town home to the city. From 1973 to 2007, it was run as a small boutique museum, a kind of giant doll's house, packed with mannequins striking poses.

When the city needed a space for a holocaust and genocide memorial centre, the decision was taken to move the dresses to Museum Africa and demolish the old museum. But since Museum Africa did not have a fashion curator, for the following ten years the garments hung in the museum vault in row after row of impeccably numbered airtight bags.

A new curator was hired in 2017, but even he is realistic about how much of the collection is ever likely to come under public gaze. Some of the garments are so old and fragile they will probably have to remain permanently in storage, while the collection of gloves, necklaces, shoes, hats, handbags, fans and dress patterns is so enormous it would probably take the entire floor space of Museum Africa to show it all.

Instead, More plans to arrange niche exhibitions, while the larger collection is available, by appointment to the city's fashion, textile and design students so that they can create new frocks of fancy, drawn from this rich city treasure trove.

"It's a collection comparable to that of the V&A Museum in London."
(Pholoso More, fashion curator of Museum Africa).

DIAZ CROSS

South Africa's oldest monument

Foyer of William Cullen Library
University of Witwatersrand (Wits)
Open: Monday — Friday 9am — 5pm. Closed weekends.

On Monday 12 March 1488, Portuguese navigator Bartholomew Diaz erected a stone cross — the 'Padrao de Sao Gregorio' — at what is now known as Kwaaihoek, at the mouth of the Bushman's River in the Eastern Cape.

Diaz and his fleet of three ships (two caravels and a square-rigged store ship) had been seeking a route to India, although they turned back after planting this cross. Diaz is believed to have been the first European to set foot on South African soil.

Diaz's cross, planted on a sandy promontory, was swallowed by time; by the 19th century, no traces of it remained. Navigators and academics argued about its original placement, but the truth remained undiscovered until 1938.

Dr. Eric Axelson, an ambitious historian, had spent two years in Europe studying the documents of the Portuguese explorers of the 15th century. His studies had led him to archives and libraries in Lisbon, Porto, the Vatican, Paris and the British Museum in London. When his ship berthed in Port Elizabeth, he drove that same day to Kwaaihoek in search of the Diaz cross.

At first look, he found nothing. But within a couple of weeks, he began an archaeological excavation, funded by Wits university, which revealed fragments of limestone unlike any other stone found naturally in that area. Over time, 5,000 fragments of the original cross were found.

With the help of a watercolour sketch of another Diaz Cross, done by one Captain Thompson of the *HMS Nautilus* in his personal journal of 1786 — a journal that Axelson found in a collection of Africana owned by Quentin Keynes, the great-grandson to Charles Darwin — the historian was able to reconstruct the cross.

Today, at Kwaaihoek, a replica overlooks the Indian Ocean, while unknown to most, the patchworked original is kept in a glass box, placed on parquet flooring beneath a chandelier in the foyer of the William Cullen Library at Wits.

However, if you had come looking for the Diaz cross in 2016, you wouldn't have found it.

During the *#FeesMustFall* student protests at the University of Witwatersrand (when students demanded that the ANC government deliver on their promise of free education, and began to agitate for the removal of colonial statues) the Diaz Cross was hidden behind paper and sticky tape after one student complained that it was an offensive symbol of colonial settlement. How long it stays on show is up for debate.

OLD PROTEST TREASURES

Objects of defiance

Historical Papers research archive
William Cullen Library
University of Witwatersrand
Open: Monday — Friday 9am — 5pm

It is an uncomfortable truth that all of the state documents that were classified during the apartheid era remain classified to this day. If you were once an anti-apartheid activist, followed and spied upon by the state apparatchik, you have to submit a Freedom of Information request to access your file. The official secrets remain officially secret.

There is, however, one place where many objects of apartheid defiance are stored — and accessible. In the 1980s, Michele Pickover, the now retired archivist at Wits, consciously began to transform the wooden drawers in this wing of the William Cullen Library into a record of activism.

Her actions were illegal. During the eighties, it was forbidden to store material that challenged the authority of the state. But Pickover would clandestinely accept documents that no other archives would host.

Among the once contraband goods are posters from the End Conscription Campaign, with slogans such as "Namibia. South Africa's Vietnam", "No to Botha's Army. Don't Vote" and "A Civil War is not very relaxing". There are also trial papers from the David Webster inquest

(Webster was assassinated by apartheid security forces in 1989), along with evidence and speeches from the infamous Rivonia Trial that saw Mandela and seven others sentenced to life imprisonment. Among the gems are Mandela's draft of his defence statement, handwritten notes which he intended to use if he was sentenced to death and his "I am prepared to die" speech, with handwritten edits in blue pen, signed by all eight defendants.

Collected more recently, are the records of the Koinonia movement: in the 1980s, small racially mixed groups would meet in each other's homes to share a meal and break down the barrier between races.

Another treasure on the walls of the archive is an extract from a speech once made by Pickover — "Archives, whether spaces or records, are continually transforming and shifting in meaning. They are fundamentally political in nature and as such are mediated sites of power, ideology and memory … a means of excavating silences."

In 2016, a new narrative began to emerge in South Africa. Many of the youth, frustrated by the continued difficult economic conditions experienced by most black South Africans, began to label Nelson Mandela as a sell-out and label all white South Africans as unreconstructed racists.

The buried papers in this fascinating archive, however, are a crucial resource for reminding every South African how diverse, difficult and determined the fight against apartheid was, how the truth is much more nuanced than we might want to believe, and how the struggle against injustice is bigger than any one of us.

A COLLECTION OF 16TH, 17TH AND 18TH CENTURY HARPSICHORDS

A treasure trove for the musical zealot

Wits School of Art
Open: By appointment only
Tel: 011-717-4616

Behind a locked door in an unmarked storeroom in the Wits School of Art is an unusual collection of keyboard instruments.

Among the collection are a 16th century Italian harpsicord, known as the Landowska, with a painted insert attributed to Verrocchio, a 17th century Bertolotti harpsichord with a Flemish painting on the wing, and an 18th century Broadwood piano. All were donated to the university by a Jewish immigrant called Hans Adler.

Raised in a home filled with music, Adler's mother had performed with Brahms and Tchaikovsky, and his first piano teacher was a pupil of Clara Schumann. He brought his love of music with him when he immigrated to South Africa in 1933. During his lifetime he was responsible for bringing many international classical artists to perform in South Africa, including the opera singer Victoria de los Angeles and the modernist composer Karlheinz Stockhausen.

In 1978, in recognition of decades-long service to music, Wits awarded Adler with an honorary doctorate. His wish in donating part of his collection was, as his widow Gertrud Adler wrote, "to inspire future generations of music students and lovers of music."

Kept under lock and key for safety and preservation purposes, the instruments can be viewed by appointment. "Their real value is as undisturbed historical objects rather than as playable instruments," explains Donato Somma, a Wits music lecturer.

Creating musical instruments to match the sound that Bach or Mozart would have heard

Recently, a genre of organology called 'historically informed performance practice' has emerged. The aim is to create musical instruments that can match the exact sound that Bach or Mozart would have heard. When musicians perform scores on these instruments, they learn something new about the way the music was intended to be heard by its composers. "It's much more visceral on these old instruments. You can hear the wood and the materials. It's a warmer and more interesting sound," says Somma.

Think of it a bit like listening to music on vinyl versus a digital download. In order to recreate these instruments, organologists need to understand the chemical composition of the varnishes, resins and glues that would have been used in the 16th, 17th and 18th centuries. In Europe, it is an increasingly difficult task to recreate the old instruments because most harpsichords and clavichords of this age have been frequently played, and thus restored with more modern resins, glues and varnishes. But this unrestored, little-played collection locked behind a Jo'burg door is a treasure trove for the musical zealot. Who would have thought?

KERK STREET MOSQUE

⑦

A gateway to Mecca

Kerk Street
Open: 5am—8am; noon—2pm; 5pm—9pm

The security guard regards anyone who tries to enter the Kerk Street Mosque outside of prayer time with suspicion. The gate is firmly locked and no amount of cajoling can convince him to let you in.

Return during the hours of prayer, and if you are not a member of the Sunni Muslim community, you will need to ask to be shown around by Yusef Twaha Asidi, one of the two moazzins who call people to prayer fives times per day. It is worth the visit.

Set deep in the downtown financial district, the Kerk Street Mosque is one of the most peaceful places within the city.

The current mosque is the third incarnation on the same site. The first, a wood and iron building, was erected in 1906. The second, a two storey building with a three-tiered minaret, served the community from 1918 until the late 1980s, when it became too small. The Muslim community then approached the National Monuments Council requesting to demolish the building and build a larger mosque. But the council refused the demolition and recommended that it be declared a national monument.

In reply, the Juma Masgied Society (the mosque trustees) wrote, "In Islam, the purpose of buildings are their need and not historic, monumental or aesthetic splendour."

The trustees won out, the old building was demolished and in its place rose up a simple white building, whose exterior gives away no clues to the treasures inside.

The mosque is set over three floors: the vestibules are adorned with the exquisite, intricate tile work of North Africa, the main prayer area soars up into a dome, and the bare white walls are decorated with beautifully carved inlays, completed by North African plasterers.

Brass chandeliers hang from the tall ceiling, carved arches soar into the heavens, and light pours in from tall windows. Latticed dark wood balconies and deep maroon, floral Persian carpets are the final touches to create a place of peace and silence.

That said, it is not a place where just anyone can find respite from the pace of the street. "We welcome people to learn about Islam," says Yusef Twaha Asidi when asked if people are welcome to just come and sit here, as one often can in a church. He is pragmatic about the reason though.

"Safety is our main concern. Outside of prayer times, the mosque is locked. We cannot just let anybody in."

OLD JOHANNESBURG STOCK EXCHANGE TRADING FLOOR

An abandoned cathedral to capitalism

Ntemi Piliso Street
Newtown
Open: By appointment only
Tel: 011-834-8221

On the lower level of the old Johannesburg Stock Exchange (JSE) building, behind locked doors and a darkened foyer in which hangs Troye's map of the Transvaal Republic, is one of the last manual stock exchange trading floors in the world.

The old JSE is almost exactly as it was left on 26 June 1996, the day that brokers made their last trade before moving to a computerised trading floor in Sandton. Look closely and you can see white darts spearing the roof and walls. The brokers rolled up the pieces of paper from their last ever trade, attached them to a dart and threw them skywards, before leaving the trading floor forever.

"Nobody knows about this place," says Peter Visser, portfolio manager and right-hand to the building's owner Aubrey Goldman, who bought this Newtown edifice in the nineties, before the Stock exchange moved out. "Most people think that the old Stock Exchange was in the diamond building next door, but that was De Beers."

Above the entrance doors hang the chalkboards on which the stock prices were scrawled, and the red and green lights which would tell you if the stock closed at a higher or lower price the previous day. At the back of the trading floor are five stained glass windows, each dedicated to a different bastion of wealth generation: agriculture, mining, industry, commerce and transport. While up high is an observation deck where visitors used to be able to watch the frenzy of the brokers at work.

The trading floor has had few visitors over the last 20 years — save for the occasional advertising shoot — and the building's owner is still contemplating what to do with this vast, somewhat gloomy chamber. Currently the ten storey building above, with its Sun City-esque internal red and glass lifts, is office space to insurance companies, private brokers, colleges and an organised crime unit. Out front is one of the few remaining green spaces in the inner city, with plans to extend it and make a pedestrianised green corridor connecting Newtown with the First National Bank inner city campus.

Like so much of inner city Jo'burg, it's an old story in search of a new ending.

ANGLO AMERICAN DOORS

A symbol of prosperity and status

44 Main Street
Marshalltown

What do the bronzed doors of Anglo American's headquarters have in common with the great gates of Buckingham Palace? Or with the great doors of the Grand Temple at the Masonic Peace Memorial in London? Or the bronze doors to the dining rooms of the Queen Mary, the Cunard White Star ocean liner (now a floating hotel at Long Beach, California)?

Answer: they were all created by the same artist, British architectural sculptor Walter Gilbert.

Gilbert had been a pupil of Benjamin Creswick, who himself had been trained by thinker, watercolourist and art critic John Ruskin, who argued that the principle role of the artist is "truth to nature". The essence of Ruskin's teaching, which became the foundation of Gilbert's work, was to examine the way the artisans of old had worked, and how they strived to create sculpted buildings that connected with their surroundings and told a story.

Inspired by the old palaces and churches of Europe and ancient India, Gilbert became known for adorning buildings with decorations that spoke to their surroundings.

Anglo American moved to the building in 1939 and remained here throughout the nineties when many inner city businesses fled to the northern suburbs. Gilbert's task was to create a fitting entrance to what was then the wealthiest mining company in the world.

The seven glazed bronzed doors at Anglo comment on the company's place in South Africa.

Above the doors is the figure of a woman holding a bridle in her hand — meant to represent prudence. At her side is a serpent, the symbol of wisdom, and at her feet, a dove.

Within the doors are the emblems of the sun (a symbol of South Africa's prosperity and wealth) and the eland and the giant sable antelope (symbols of her great and unusual possessions). The storks and swallows flying outwards symbolise her travel and trade with other parts of the world, while the eagles were chosen for the door handles as symbols of power and beauty.

Gilbert, in collaboration with his son Donald, also created the doors for the entrances on Marshall and Ferreira Streets, where the design takes a more subtle turn; the delicate ribbing on the doors meant to evoke that seen on the wing of a South African butterfly.

MASTERPIECES IN THE MAGISTRATE'S COURT

⑩

Hidden in plain sight

Johannesburg Magistrate's Court
Corner of Fox and Ntemi Piliso Streets
Ferreirasdorp
Transport: Take the Rea Vaya C3 route. Exit at the Carlton Centre on Commissioner Street. Head west towards Kruis Street then turn left on to Ntemi Piliso.
Open: Monday—Friday 8am—3:30pm

Overlooked by most visitors and employees, two large and beautiful paintings hang opposite each other across a stairwell in the Johannesburg Magistrate's Court. One depicts Johannesburg as a mining village in 1886, the other a more developed cityscape of the 1930s.

To the untrained eye, these paintings may appear as mere illustrations of the city's history. But look closely at the emotive skies, flat geometric planes of the (natural and manmade) landscape and the formalised composition and you might recognise the brushwork of an old master.

Jacobus Hendrik Pierneef is considered one of the South Africa's most influential artists. He was commissioned to paint the pieces in 1940 to commemorate the opening of the court. Unfortunately, the 4.3m x 5.4m paintings are hung at an inconvenient height for viewing.

It's only if you happen to turn back and look down on them from the top of the stairs that you get a decent view. But most people are too busy scurrying to or from court to pay much attention.

Julian Gous, a fine art restorer who was commissioned to restore the paintings at the Magistrate's Court in 1987 and again in 2012, told *The Star* newspaper in 2012, "Most people don't even notice the paintings are there. Others think I'm the artist [working on a new project] so they stop to compliment me."

The paintings' anonymity may well be their saving grace. In June 2017, the auctioneers Straus & Co. sold the previously unseen Pierneef *Farm Jonkershoek with Twin Peaks Beyond, Stellenbosch* for a record R20 million. The painting is a fraction of the size of the Pierneefs in the Magistrate's Court, which have hung opposite each other for nearly 80 years.

"No one knows they are there, and the people who notice them don't know the value of what they are looking at," says a Magistrate at the court. "They had a burglary a while back and the computers were stolen. I reckon the thieves would have been better off taking the Pierneefs."

In a nod to Johannesburg's more recent history, a sculpture of Nelson Mandela by Marco CIanfanelli, *Shadow Boxing* (2013), was installed on Fox Street between the court and Chancellor House — the law practice shared by Mandela and Oliver Tambo, and the first African law practice in South Africa. The offices have been preserved as an informal street museum with information and photographs displayed in the windows.

THE STRANGE STACKS

A place we should know better

Johannesburg Public Library
Beyers Naudé Square
Open: Monday—Friday 9am—5pm; Saturday 9am—1pm
Tel: 011-022-0916 (Elton) to book a tour

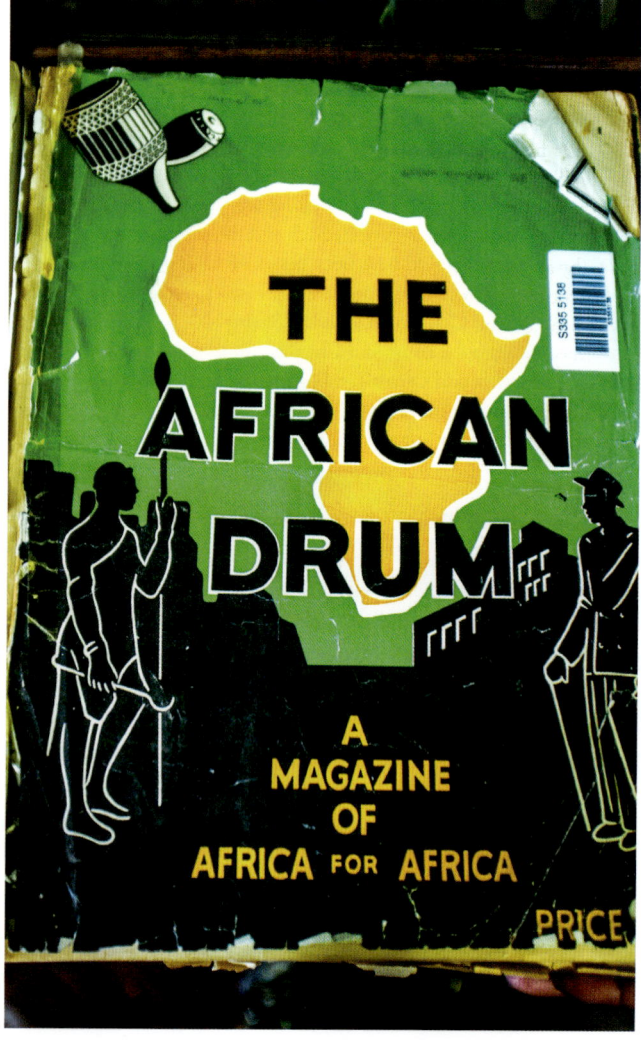

One of the most inspiring statues in downtown Johannesburg must be the woman in Beyers Naudé square — a baby strapped to her back, holding a petrol bomb in one hand and a placard with the words "Democracy is Dialogue" in the other. Made by artist Lawrence Lemaoana, the statue is dedicated to all the women who have for decades fought for social and political change.

The inspiration runs still deeper; four storey's deep in fact, into the earth beneath Beyers Naudé Square. It is here, stretching all the way from Sauer to Simmonds Streets, that the Johannesburg Public Library has its stacks, bookshelf after bookshelf in the bowels of the earth, storing the most extraordinary treasures. Ever wished you could get your hands on a copy of *The Star* newspaper from the day you were born? Or firemen's records from the 1930s? Fancy reading the log of the *HMS Bounty*? Or how about the gospel of St. Luke in Tswana? Or Tolstoy in Russian?

"We throw nothing away," says Elton, reference librarian who offers tours (by appointment) into this warm and humid underground world, where the temperature is set to suit paper, rather than people. "Not many people know about the treasures we have here. I learn something new every day."

Among the most interesting is the overspill of the Strange Library, the city's collection of Africana books. In the early 20th century it became fashionable to collect books about Africa, and Harold Strange, who became the President of the Transvaal Chamber of Mines and president of the Wanderers club, was an avid collector. Much of his collection was purchased from booksellers in London and Amsterdam, and when he died in 1912, the library bought the collection.

From then on it has grown enormously, with books collected from all over Africa up to the 1960s then from authors from Botswana, Mozambique, Zimbabwe, Malawi and Namibia up to the early 1990s. During apartheid, when many books were banned, the library would still buy the banned books.

"They would buy them and then lock them away," says Linda, former librarian at the Strange.

Sadly due to budget re-prioritising, many of the books written in the post-apartheid era are not included in the Strange Library. And today, when budget is allocated for book buying, the priority is to purchase books written in the vernacular languages of South Africa.

ROCK ART OF THE VOLK
⑫

A history etched in granite

External wall of the old Volkskas HQ
Albertina Sisulu Street

South Africa is reknown for its rock art — a symbolic art form carved into cave walls by the San Bushmen, often telling stories of spirit world journeys and experiences of the San shamans.

Normally something you would expect to find on a hike through the Drakensberg mountains, the external wall of the Department of Infrastructure & Development — formerly the headquarters of the Volkskas Bank — could stop you in your tracks.

In the early 1920s, there was a growing opinion among Afrikaner leaders that something had to be done to improve the economic position of Afrikaners, who had been impoverished by the South African War. The Afrikaner Broederbond came up with the concept of 'volkskapitalisme' — people's capitalism. In 1934, Volkskas (the People's Treasury) was established as a co-operative bank through which Afrikaners could pool together their savings to counter the pressures of foreign capitalism.

Sculptor Willem de Sanderes Hendrikz was commissioned by Volkskas to create art for the exterior of the Johannesburg head office, which was next door to the head office of the Broederbond. The art was intended to commemorate "the dawn of volk economic consciousness", establishing a visual connection between the past and the ideal of the economic empowerment of Afrikaners. At the time of its construction the building was considered to be the first major piece of architecture to be erected in Johannesburg by the emergent forces of Afrikaner finance capital.

Hendrikz's first panel is of an African woman surveying the bounty of nature. In the following panel, Jan van Riebeek appears as an overlord to the native Africans. The panels continue from left to right, telling the story of the Afrikaner progression, from small-scale farming to mining and industrialization. He also created the bronze front doors and the mosaic on the threshold to the building, which reads "Arbeidsaamheid" (meaning 'unity in work').

Hendrikz engraved the panels in situ and eventually requested temporary screens to be erected on the pavement while he was working because people kept stopping to admire his craftsmanship. Being shy, he felt uncomfortable with all the attention. He probably wouldn't have to worry if he was there today, with most people watching their backs and their bags as they make their way through downtown Jo'burg.

THE LIGHTHOUSE IN THE SKY

A beacon in a dark time

Security Building
95 Commissioner Street

Stand at the corner of Commissioner and Simmonds Streets and look up. A block away, silhouetted against the sky, is the city's only lighthouse, perched on top of the Security Building.

Designed in 1935 by J. Lockwood Hall, the architect also responsible for the Pretoria City Hall and the Benoni Town Hall, the *raison d'être* for the lighthouse has faded from collective memory, though there is a likely explanation.

In 1931, Lockwood Hall designed a building in East London for the Tower Building Society, which had a lighthouse as its logo.

"It was probably the symbol of light in a storm for investors or property owners," says East London-based architect William Martinson. That building later became known as the Standard Building, and later still, the Security Building, the same name as that sported by the Jo'burg lighthouse.

According to a National Monuments Act letter dated 16 August 1989, there is mention of equipment that was used to operate the lighthouse, although no traces remain today.

However, it wasn't just the lighthouse that made this building unique. During apartheid, it was home to the Jameson's Bar, one of the bars in the city that had a Kruger License — a liquor license issued by Paul Kruger at the turn of the 20th century that permitted black and white people to drink in the space.

Describing Jameson's Bar in his book *Voelvry: The Movement that Rocked South Africa,* detailing the underground protest scene in South Africa, author Pat Hopkins wrote, "It was a dim and dirty enclave. Descending those stairs felt like a descent into the underworld. Young (mostly white) South Africans mixed with their counterparts of colour; everyone got trashed together. It was like the bastard child of Sophiatown. It was the new South Africa in a twisted embryo."

The lighthouse flirted with fame again in 2010 when the 10th floor of the building briefly became a nightclub with the intention of bringing back the underground house, break beat and funk scene in Jozi, reminiscent of late 1990s house music clubs such as 115, Therapy, Gas, and Reality, though it didn't last long.

Today, the building is owned by Urban Ocean Property Developers and is one of many in the inner city earmarked for redevelopment.

"We're considering re-establishing the Jameson Bar," says CEO Herman Schoeman.

For the time being though, the lighthouse though will remain a dark phantom.

ROCKFACE

A waterfall in the concrete jungle

28 Harrison Street
Open: During office hours

Downtown Jo'burg is a bit like Marmite, you either love it or you hate it. Those that despise it often describe it as too intense, a place where you are constantly pushing forward, while always watching your back, without any place to relax. That said, there is an unexpected oasis of calm on the corner of Fox and Harrison.

In 1993, mining giant JCI commissioned a new downtown headquarters. No expense was spared and architect Robin Fee envisioned a "Prospero's Palace'", incorporating a façade of Baltic Brown granite imported from a quarry on the border of Finland and Russia.

The building was earmarked for the south-east corner of the intersection of Fox and Harrison, but plans were hampered when the owners of Equity House, a small old building on the very corner of the stand, refused to sell. Not put off, JCI decided to build their new headquarters around this old edifice, and Fee came up with the idea of turning the back of the building, which would protrude into their new lobby, into a water wall.

Fee approached Mickey Korzennik, a sculptor of Jewish-Lithuanian and Austro-Hungarian extraction who was born in Cape Town in 1930. Korzennik came up with the idea of a four-storey waterfall made of 25 tons of cast stainless steel, which he named Rockface. His idea was to bring an artist's interpretation of an underground mine into the lobby of the mining house, as if peeling back the granite to reveal the scoured rock face deep below the earth, pockmarked by miners digging for gold.

According to Korzennik, the waterfall was such an expensive undertaking that Robin Fee had to get the head of Anglo American Property Services (the developing arm handling the project) drunk to agree to the price. But even four bottles of wine were not enough to extract a yes, and the decision had to be taken to the very top, requiring Gordon Waddel, then managing director of JCI, to sign off the ambitious project.

The waterfall took nine months to build and install, and although JCI are long gone — the building is now rented as mixed-use offices — the waterfall remains, framed by ferns and surrounded by benches, making it one of the most inviting and safe sanctuaries of calm inside the incessant pulse of the inner city.

CORNER HOUSE'S CUPOLA ⑮

A lucky charm for the city

Corner of Commissioner and Simmonds Streets
Open: Access during office hours

On the corner of Commissioner and Simmonds is one of the oldest buildings in the city — and a testament to its gold mining wealth. Begun in 1886 as a single-storey wood and iron shack, rebuilt in 1890 and again in 1905, this ten storey ornate edifice was where gold mining prospectors would come to acquire the capital required to fund the stamp batteries, access to water, and the amalgam plates required to turn a gold prospect into a profitable mine. At the time it was built, it was the largest and tallest commercial building in South Africa.

For many decades the Corner House remained a symbol of financial power in southern Africa. Like many inner-city buildings, it went through a period of abandonment. But in recent years it has been restored and reinvented by property developers Urban Ocean.

To many, though, it remains an emblem of South African capitalism, which makes it somewhat ironic that the Economic Freedom Fighters (the anti-capitalism political party determined to overthrow the establishment and redistribute land and wealth to the people) have their offices here.

The EFF are not the only surprise within the building: the entrance foyer boasts original arts and crafts tiles dating back to 1903, the first floor offices are panelled with Burmese teak, the rooftop houses a copper dome and a private venue that can be hired for functions, and the ground floor has a cool-as-you-like co-working space, popular with advertising creatives. It also has a hairdresser.

The most beguiling treasure, however, might be the magnificent coloured glass cupola in the foyer of the Simmonds Street entrance.

This domed ceiling is edged with bas-reliefs of two gold merchant adventurer ships and two incarnations of Tyche (also called Fortuna), who was the goddess of fortune and prosperity in a mythological Greek city. Tyche is often depicted wearing a crown made of city walls. Poignantly, she was often shown on Greek vases standing alongside Nemesis, the goddess of retribution and revenge, who would show her wrath to any human being that would commit arrogance before the gods.

There is no sign of Nemesis on the cupola, but her modern incarnation can probably be found on the second floor, wearing a red beret.

CUTHBERT'S CUPOLA

⑯

A mini Maboneng of its day

Rooftop of Cuthberts Building
Corner of Pritchard and Eloff Streets
Open: By appointment only
Tel: 082-904-2813 (heritage consultant Brian McKechnie)

When Jonathan Liebemann (the entrepreneur whose vision kickstarted the Maboneng art precinct) tied the knot, he chose a Victorian pavilion perched on top of a derelict inner-city building for the ceremony.

Designed by architects Stucke & Bannister and built in 1904, the pavilion was once the crowning glory of the flagship store of Cuthberts, the shoe merchant.

During the city's heyday in the 1920s and 1930s, Cuthberts' Victorian cast-ironwork made it one of the most beautiful buildings in Jo'burg. Its first floor tearoom — called the Corner Lounge — was the place to see and be seen. After a morning of retail therapy, people would stop in to listen to jazz. It was also during those years that the rooftop pavilion became an artist studio.

The studio's first occupant was J.H. Amshewitz, the son of a Rabbi who had studied at the Royal Academy in England and won commissions for murals in Liverpool's City Halls before arriving in South Africa. Amshewitz first rented 'The Dome', as he called it, in 1916 (the same year he started the Johannesburg Sketch Club), and later again in 1936 when he returned to South Africa after a stint back in England. Over the course of his career he was also a cartoonist for the Rand *Daily Mail* and *Sunday Times*, and became a mentor to other artists.

Another artist who used the pavilion as her studio was Emily Fern, an associate of Amshewitz who had been one of the first students to enrol at the Johannesburg School of Art in 1913. Fern had been first taught to paint by a nun at the End Street Convent, and later studied at the Slade School of Art in London, She went on to study in Paris under Andre Lhote, the French Cubist whose figurative style influenced a whole generation of painters.

Fern became known for her portraits of black South Africans, which moved away from racial stereotyping, instead attempting to reveal the deep psychology of the people at the end of her brush.

In 1986, the Cuthberts Building was declared a National Monument, but like so many other inner-city buildings, it became derelict during the early 2000s.

Today the cupola stands empty, but Liebemann has bought the building. Given time, perhaps it will once again become an artistic home for another generation of creatives.

CECILY SASH MOSAIC IN LITTLE ETHIOPIA

A prominent artwork lost in a new world

Haile Selassie Centre
220 Rahima Moosa Street
Johannesburg city centre

Little Addis or Little Ethiopia, as the area around 220 Rahima Moosa Street is colloquially known, is frothing with industry. The multi-storey building is a warren of small shops crammed with shoes, incense, spices, coffee beans, hats, traditional Ethiopian garb, CDs, religious paraphernalia and Rastafarian souvenirs.

As you head up the stairs, you'll be hit by the contrasting aromas of strong coffee and the sour-sweet smell of injeera, a traditional spongy flatbread that is enjoyed with a fragrant variety of stews and salads.

Among the throng, in what used to be the reception to the building, is a dull, curved marble bench and bright mosaic that hint at a very different era. The centre's previous incantation was as the Medical Arts Building, and the once plush foyer was the first port of call before visiting some of Johannesburg's top medical specialists.

The mosaic, depicting an abstracted agrarian African scene, is frequently hidden behind packing boxes or framed Coptic Christian posters. It's a pity because the mural was created by the once popular South African artist Cecily Sash, who rose to prominence in the late 1950s and 1960s. Despite being commissioned to undertake a number of mosaics, including at Jan Smuts Airport (now O.R. Tambo International), this is one of few remaining large-scale public works.

If you consider the premise behind this period of Sash's work, it's apt that the mosaic has survived the building's transition from a well-off whites-only enclave to a pulsing cosmopolitan hub.

Sash was part of the Amadlozi (meaning "spirit of our ancestors") group, a loose collective of artists in the 1960s who sought to express the essence of Africa in distinct ways. Traditionally, white South African modernists had appropriated African imagery and shoehorned it into a distinctly European aesthetic. The Amadlozi, however, aimed to create a uniquely South African form of modernism that spoke to cultural inclusion and exhibited along non-racial lines.

The appropriation of the building as an Ethiopian landmark began in the mid-1990s after democracy (and Nelson Mandela in particular), made South Africa an appealing destination for immigrants from the rest of Africa. A single Ethiopian restaurant was opened at the front of the building and became the go-to place for Ethiopian newcomers to get tips on how to survive their new home. Over time the community grew and more Ethiopian businesses were established in the building and surrounding area.

THE SPACESHIP MAST

⑱

Back to the future

Anstey's Building
Corner of Jeppe and Joubert Streets
Open: By appointment
Tel: 082-904-2813 (Heritage consultant Brian McKechnie)

Anstey's is one of the city's most famous Art Deco buildings. Built on the site of some 19th century tennis courts belonging to the Johannesburg Tennis Club, for a time after its completion in 1937 it was the second highest building in Africa.

Throughout much of the last century, Anstey's was the address. Its first four floors were home to the city's swankiest department store, Norman Anstey and Company, while the penthouse was where the chairman of the Johannesburg Stock Exchange laid his head. It was also home to some illustrious political figures.

Cecil Williams, the actor, playwright and member of Umkhonto we Sizwe, lived here. Nelson Mandela was posing as his chauffeur in order to travel around the country holding political conversations when he was captured on 5 August 1962.

But it's up on the roof that Anstey's keeps its abiding secret resident. Poking up into the sky, keeping pace with the skyscrapers of Jo'burg is a sturdy mast. At first glance it may look like a radio mast, but this antenna is an alternative version of a helicopter landing pad, for a future that has yet to arrive.

"When Anstey's was built in the 1930s, people were obsessed with the idea of creating cities of the future. The architects (Emley & Williamson) envisioned a time when people would arrive at the building by spaceship or blimp. The idea that people would tether their blimps to the mast and then let down a ladder to arrive at the building from the sky," says Brian McKechnie, an architect and heritage consultant who owns a number of flats in the building.

Over the decades the building's fortunes shifted — "Anstey lost the building to gambling debts," says McKechnie — and by 1989, Anstey's was earmarked for demolition. The destruction never happened. By 1995 its fortune had shifted again and it was listed as a National Monument.

Today the building is almost entirely residential, housing tenants from all walks of life. Some flats have interiors that would not look out of place in a glossy magazine. Others are simple homes that meet the needs of those looking for low-cost accommodation. There is also a floor dedicated to artists' studios, a health clinic, and a roof terrace that the residents use as a chill-out space, still waiting for their spaceship to arrive.

TRANSNET'S MYSTERY ARCHIVE ⑲
A treasure trove of railway heritage

Knowledge Centre
96 Rissik Street
Open: Contact Yolanda Meyer for appointments
Tel: 011-773-8726

The political sea change that has happened since 1994 has meant that Jo'burg is often a stranger to itself. And there's perhaps no better example of this than the heritage library of Transnet, the South African railway company, which is a mystery even to the librarian who runs it.

Even before the days of the gold and diamond mining boom, this government-linked railway company has always kept an in-house library. In the early days, when European engineers were constructing new railways that would connect South African commodities to ports and markets, it would take two months for journals and information about new engineering developments to arrive by ship from Europe. The railway's library became a critical hub of knowledge on how to build everything from scratch.

In the early 1980s, it was decided to split this resource in two. Everything post-1960 would become a Knowledge Centre run by Freight Rail, and all pre-1960 information would form a heritage library and museum run by the Transnet Foundation.

In the 2000s, the head of the Transnet Foundation, who also ran the Phelophepa "train of hope" that delivered much-needed medical services to rural and impoverished communities, decided there was no need to keep the heritage library going.

The museum artefacts were sent to railway museums in George and Kimberley, staff were retrenched, and the instruction was given for all the books, journals, travel posters and some 250,000 photographs to be thrown away.

When word reached the ears of railway enthusiasts, hearts stopped. The Knowledge Centre was asked to intervene, but it was too late. All of the computer servers that indexed the collection were gone. All the information on how to find anything was lost forever.

Today, in the bowels of the Transnet building, an unsearchable collection of railway heritage fills room after room.

"It is always a surprise when I open a drawer," says information specialist, Yolanda Meyer.

In one folder, the timetable for the funeral train that delivered Cecil John Rhodes's body from Cape Town to Bulawayo; in another the lantern slides of South African scenes that were once sent to embassies to promote the beauty of the country abroad; in another, sound recordings of old steam locomotives.

It is a story, however, that does have a happy ending. Today, a group of volunteer fundraisers employ young, out-of-work South Africans to reclassify and digitise this resource. And Meyer welcomes anyone who wants to volunteer to put this piece of the past, back in order.

"If you don't know where you come from, you won't know where you are going," she says.

LARRY SCULLY MURALS

A secret cityscape

Student Diggz
Dudley Heights
11 Hospital Street
Braamfontein
Open: By appointment only
Tel: 078-258-0865 (Erin)

The Jo'burg skyline is as loved as Table Mountain, the unchanging backdrop to our constantly changing city. There are plenty of great vantage points to see the skyline — Langerman's Kop in Kensington is a top spot — but there is an alternative vista tucked away in the bowels of a Braamfontein apartment block.

In the 1960s, when the city was in the throes of a building spree, the father of Linda Goodman (the well known artist and founder of the Goodman Gallery) built the Dudley Heights apartment block. Goodman Snr. commissioned artist Larry Scully, who later produced the "Madonna and Child of Soweto" hanging in the Regina Mundi church in Soweto, to create a mural for the lobby. Scully went on to become Head of Fine Arts at the Johannesburg College of Education.

Scully's vision was to create a modernist landscape of Jo'burg, as if it was a city of the future.

"It was one of the most ambitious commissions of the time," says Karel Nel, artist and Professor of Art at Wits University. "The lobby was even made taller to make the murals more powerful."

Scully used an innovative technique for his murals. Look carefully and you will see that part of the mural is done on canvas and glued to the wall, while the rest is painted in situ. He also used gravity to create the runs. The shimmering colours on black backdrops were meant to represent the drama of the city, the glitter of electric light, and the endless space and light of Africa, just beyond the perimeter of the concrete jungle.

Born in England, Scully came as a young man to South Africa and moved up through the ranks of the art world. In the 1970s, motivated by a strong political conscience, he organised the Johannesburg Biennale. His intention was to have all South Africans represented as artists and audience members. The week before the exhibition was to open, Scully was ordered by the South African government to limit the biennale to whites only. He cancelled the event.

Today Dudley Heights is part of Student Digzz, an inner city student residence popular with those studying photography and design. The entrance is no longer through the old lobby but Scully's murals have found a new *raison d'etre*: they have become the backdrop to a space that students are being encouraged to use to host pop-up exhibitions and express their emerging creativity.

WINDYBROW

A mansion that has survived against all odds

Corner of Nugget and Pietersen Streets
Doornfontein
Open: By appointment only
Tel: 011-832-1641

The three carved mythological gods guarding the entrance to Windybrow seem as out of place as the building itself.

In the early days of the gold mining boom, Doornfontein was *the* address for Jo'burg's mining magnates. In 1896, Theodore Reunert, the man later responsible for the electrification of the cities of Port Elizabeth and East London, commissioned this Anglo Moorish house from the architect William Leck. Named Windybrow after romantic poet Robert Southey's home in the English Lake District (whose poems Reunert was reportedly reading at the time), the mansion was, and still is, a feast for the eyes: Moorish tiled fireplaces in every room, intricate wood panelling, walls embossed with peacocks, flowers and grapes, and a Shakespeare quote carved in Art Nouveau script in the entrance hall — *"Welcome ever smile and farewell goes out sighing"*.

As is the nature of this city, constantly in flux, Doornfontein later fell out of favour with the super wealthy — all of them relocating to new mansions in Parktown — and Windybrow was turned first into a barracks for an English general, and later into the city's first college of nursing, while its neighbouring mansions were knocked down to make way for industrial units and functional apartment blocks.

In the 1980s, Windybrow went through another makeover, becoming a theatre for the bohemian, politically astute residents of Hillbrow. It was here that many black artists began their careers. Sadly, post 1994, a sorry tale of mismanagement and potential fraud saw the building fall into disrepair – R66 million is still missing, with the South African special investigations unit, the Hawks, showing no interest in investigating.

However, the fate of Windybrow is changing once again. In 2015, the Department of Arts and Culture ordered the successful Market Theatre to take over the management and renovation of the house.

"When I tell people what we are doing, they usually say: 'I didn't even know it still existed'," remarks the Market Theatre's Christine McDonald. "I once asked a homeless man who has sat on this road for the past ten years what he knows about it. He said he had never heard of it."

Their aim is not to gentrify, but to turn this glorious old dame into a community theatre, co-working space and arts centre; a place for collaboration and creativity in a part of the city where day-to-day survival is more often at the top of people's agenda.

POETRY STEPS

A flight of fancy

Nugget Street
Hillbrow

On the eastern flank of Nugget Street as it rises up from Doornfontein to Hillbrow, there is a rocky hill cut through with a flight of cement steps. The steps are engraved with the words:

"All these things that you have heard, seen, heard about, felt, smelt, believed, disbelieved, shirked, embraced, brewing in your consciousness, would find chilling, haunting echoes in the simple words ... Welcome to our Hillbrow"

The words are an extract from a book published in 2002 by writer Phaswane Mpe, which tells the story of a character who lived for five years in Hillbrow during the 1990s, when Mpe was also a resident.

It was during that decade that Hillbrow transformed from a bohemian and largely Jewish suburb to a transient arrival point for Africans from across the continent. It also became synonymous with drugs and prostitution, earning the moniker "Killbrow".

In 2008, in a bid to combat crime and renew civic pride, the City commissioned artists to reactivate public spaces that had become no-go zones.

It was a commission that sculptor Maja Marx had mixed feelings about.

"Hillbrow is a space that is being made by the people. As they move through it they are making the story of the city. Whether you like it or not, it is still an active space. It just doesn't belong to you," says Marx. "You can't force people to use it in a certain way."

Her idea then, was to borrow Mpe's words to welcome someone into the space they already used.

"It is amazing when people can walk a space, and say a space. It is not someone from the outside being welcomed, but it is someone who is already there, welcoming themselves," she says.

During the installation, Jo'burg artist Andrew Lindsay was also commissioned to create a mosaic for the hillside. In the past, a waterfall used to flow down this hill and people used to come here to have their wedding pictures taken. The waterfall has since been redirected, so in a tribute to times gone by, Lindsay created a seven-metre-high mosaic waterfall. The installation turned out to be harder than he had initially anticipated. He ended up engaging the help of the Pretoria mountaineering club, who offered their rock climbing skills for free one Sunday afternoon, to fix the mosaic to the rock face.

The end result was so admired that, perhaps fittingly for Hillbrow's reputation, the mosaic panels were stolen. Their current resting place remains yet another city secret.

MOTHER THERESA'S BLESSING ㉓

A handwritten blessing from Calcutta

Cathedral of Christ the King
186 Nugget Street
Doornfontein
Open: By appointment only

Father Thabo's face lights up at the idea of finding a secret in Johannesburg's Cathedral. There must be one in there somewhere.

To many South African Catholics, this once central cathedral, with its magnificent stained glass windows, has become something of a forgotten treasure. Once a bustling bohemian hub, this part of Doornfontein on the edge of Hillbrow has become synonymous with crime, and its past parishioners have relocated to more salubrious parts of the city.

Nowadays, its congregation tends to be a multinational mix of people from Rwanda, Kenya, Uganda, Zimbabwe, Nigeria and Congo, who have come to South Africa in search of their fortune, with Hillbrow as the first rung on the ladder to a better life.

Above the organ gallery, one of the stained glass images (a net and a fish) expresses how the church welcomes one and all — "The kingdom of heaven is like a net that was let down into the lake and caught all kinds of fish." (Matthew 13:47).

The church was designed by architect Brian Gregory from Belfast in Northern Ireland, and was consecrated in 1960. For many years the ex-serviceman's MOTH (Memorable Order of Tin Hats) club stood in its grounds, with a tank parked outside. Today, the club is a soup kitchen that serves food daily to homeless people and refugees. The tank has been replaced by a giant cross.

To find the hidden gem, ask Father Thabo to admit you to the sacristy behind the altar, where the visitors' book is kept under lock and key. Not only is there a handwritten entry from Pope John Paul VI, signed when he was still a cardinal, but a blessing — "God Bless you all" — written by Mother Teresa, who won the Nobel Peace Prize in 1979 and visited the cathedral on 14 November 1988. Mother Teresa was in South Africa to found a mission of her order, The Missionaries of Charity, in Khayelitsha, which was to serve as a home for HIV/AIDS sufferers.

Megan Mackay, a layperson who has been with the church for 54 years and runs the soup kitchen in the old Moth Club House, remembers the day Mother Teresa visited. "There were hundreds of people there. I remember that she sat with the congregation, not in the sanctuary. I was taken aback by what a little thing she was."

THE OLD VICTORIAN HOTHOUSE ㉔

The bees of Joubert Park

Wolmerans Street
Hillbrow
Email: info@ghouse.org.za
www.greenhouse.org.za

In its heyday in the late 1800s and early 1900s, Joubert Park was a place to perambulate with parasols and prams; a place to see and be seen by the upper echelons of society. It boasted a bandstand, a fountain and a clock set into a flowerbed of carefully landscaped multicoloured blossoms.

Plants and seeds were brought in from across South Africa to populate the park, and an impressive Victorian conservatory, known as the Hothouse, boasted exotic imports in temperature-controlled zones to mirror their native climates.

There was a fishpond with an impressive water lily collection, and orchids flirted and fawned in abundant clusters. Mother-in-law's tongue, delicious monsters and coffee plants vied for attention with jade vines and cyclamens, while their more stoic counterparts were set aside in a cooler, drier room for desert succulents.

The park is now a shadow of its former colonial self, but its worn pathways and scrubby lawns remain an important green space for the occupants of the high-density apartment blocks and crowded streets of Hillbrow. On any day of the week, you'll find a buzz of vendors, dealers, loafers, lovers, preachers and families. About 20,000 people use the park each month.

To the north west of the park, you'll find the ghost of the old Victorian Hothouse, now known as the Conservatory, tucked behind security fencing. She still stands tall with the deportment of a dignitary, although her eaves are tatty and many of the panes of glass that used to make her shimmer with refinement are shattered or missing. But sometimes importance is simply a matter of how you look at things. "Nowdays, people seem to see things with the eyes of scarcity, instead of with the eyes of abundance. We no longer allow ourselves to dream as human beings. I'm not sure what happened," says Itumeleng Poote, a member of the Megutung Nursery Cooperative, while he works on mysteriously shaped concrete frames under cover of the Conservatory. "To be a guy from Soweto and be able to come here from day to day is really something."

The cooperative works in partnership with the Greenhouse Project, an urban environmental NPO and training facility based on the land on which the Conservatory stands. While the Hothouse no longer boasts elegant exotics, it has been given a far more practical purpose as a food garden. What's more, it turns out the concrete frames Poote is working on are experimental prototypes for inexpensive bee boxes.

"Having bees in the city. Who would've thought that?" Asks Poote. "Even I didn't see that coming. Now that's something! Especially coming from the perspective of understanding that the African bee is vanishing in South Africa. Without the bees we risk our own extinction."

And in this way, at least, the grand old dame that is the Conservatory is still the buzz of Joubert Park.

TWIST STREET BENCH

㉕

A bench to change your perspective

Corner of Kapteijn and Twist Streets
Hillbrow
Transport: Rea Vaya C3 bus, Bathhouse stop

On the eastern edge of this busy Hillbrow thoroughfare, teeming with taxis and people hurrying to make a living and a life, is a bench with a surprising view. Stop for a moment, sit down and look up. Behind a thick stone wall, three storeys above the street, is a giant glass window through which you can watch the rehearsals of the dancers of the Outreach Foundation.

Built in the grounds of the Lutheran Church (a 120-year-old Gothic Revival sandstone structure), this slick new building, designed by architects Local Studio, already counts the Cuban Ballet and Alvin Ailey Dance Theatre among its performers. The bench was specifically situated for passers-by to pause and add a touch of art to their harried lives.

Of course, the idea of pausing for even a moment in Hillbrow is an idea too far for many South Africans. Though once Johannesburg's most bohemian suburb, where white and black intellectuals, artists and activists rubbed shoulders as the collapse of apartheid gathered speed in the late eighties, the authorities rebranded Hillbrow a "grey area" (an area with a significant illegal black, Indian and coloured population) and rumours of rising crime rates in other grey areas prompted the white residents to flee to the suburbs.

By the early nineties, many apartment blocks lay empty and the neighbourhood fell into decline. When South Africa began to relax its border controls with other African nations, these abandoned inner-city apartment blocks fell into the hands of some of Africa's most enterprising businessmen — illegal landlords, drug dealers and pimps — and the once hippest neighbourhood in Africa had become a dangerous, urban slum that soon earned the sobriquet "Killbrow".

Today, the neighbourhood is changing again. Young businessmen, many of them Jewish, have bought up the squatted buildings, turning them into safe, affordable housing for lower-income families. And it's generous donations from these same businessmen that have funded the new dance centre.

Vibrant, creative communities are good for business. Bigboy Hadebe, 18, agrees. "This place is like a second home to us. We get to express our emotions. You learn about life in this place. So many kids in Hillbrow are addicted to nyope (a drug concoction that mixes anti-retrovirals with a selection of rat poison, battery acid, cleaning detergents and marijuana). Here you get to understand who you really are."

So next time you're passing, stop for a moment and watch the next generation discovering itself.

THE GREEN OFFICE

㉖

An inner-city oasis with a military past
Drill Hall
Corner of Twist and Plein Streets

For most of the last century, the Drill Hall was a place of war. Built in 1904 to be the headquarters for the Transvaal Volunteers, it was used throughout apartheid for military drills and civilian shooting competitions in its underground firing range.

It was also here, in 1956, that Nelson Mandela, Albert Luthuli, Oliver Tambo, Walter Sisuslu and 152 other anti-apartheid activists were tried for high treason — and acquitted. It was the later Rivonia Trial that saw many of the struggle leaders sentenced to life imprisonment.

With the advent of democracy, the building was abandoned and fell into urban decay. As the inner city became home to the country's destitute, over a thousand people made their home at the Drill Hall, until two fires in 2001 and 2002 killed ten people. The disaster forced the Johannesburg Development Agency to rethink the future of this inner-city landmark, and architect Michael Hart was tasked with turning the building into a public space that could host a life skills centre (Thembalethu), an artist-run gallery (Joubert Park Project) and a library (KeleKetla!).

Despite the big ambition, the city of Johannesburg failed to maintain the building. The artists and library left, and it was into this ailing dream that Menzi Mbonambi arrived.

"The energy of the place is of military and war — it is an implanted energy that exists in this space," he says.

Menzi's remedy was to turn a corner of the building (which had become an outdoor toilet full of human waste) into a green oasis.

With like-minded souls, he began rescuing plants that had been discarded on building sites.

"We gave them a new home here. The plants bring healing to a space that has really suffered and is bruised. The plants are our saviours," he says, pointing out succulents he has rehomed in plant pots made of rubber tyres, ferns in a hanging garden constructed from an old African blanket, and living sculptures made of old tree trunks, discarded inner-city objects and flowers. He has named the garden The Green Office.

"We are trying to spread consciousness. For the city to be healed it needs guardians, people to work towards its healing."

Menzi explains how he came to think this way; "I asked myself what my great-great-grandfather, who lived before colonialism and apartheid, would have seen in Africa when he woke up," he says. "We come from the soil and we survive from the soil. I am part of the forest and we are bringing that forest back to the city."

POST OFFICE MURALS

Impressions of the past

Post Office
Jeppe Street

Unlit and overshadowed by the bright red post office branding, the murals above and behind the counters at Jeppe Street Post Office are easily overlooked. This was once the city's main, bustling post office, opened in 1935 by General J.B.M. Hertzog, then Prime Minister of the Union of South Africa.

The building was designed to impress and to symbolise the emergence of a modern state. Among its boasts were underground tunnels with state-of-the-art conveyor belts that moved mail rapidly between Park Station and the sorting room.

Today, the tunnels are derelict and the post office is being whittled back to its bare bones, while the rest of the building is being parceled off to create affordable and luxury housing, fashion stores and a supermarket.

But the murals on the public concourse have been earmarked for preservation by the city's heritage champions. This is important because they are like windows to a time that has receded from view.

In one mural, against a backdrop of orchards, mountains and clouds, a kneeling black lady is offering oranges to a seated young white lady, who is counting the oranges in her own basket. In another, a rural tribesman approaches the mines on the Witwatersrand, while a larger-than-life kneeling white man with blonde locks beckons him forth.

Painted in pale pigments, not only do they provide a window into the colonial gaze, they bare a striking similarity to the washed out landscapes of J.H. Pierneef. This work, though, is not by him but by Petrus Anton Hendriks, a Dutchman who came to South Africa in 1926 at the invitation of Pierneef. Hendriks went on to become the director of the Johannesburg Art Gallery.

Set even further back, behind the post office counters, are murals by Sydney Carter and Alfred Palmer. Carter travelled widely around South Africa, recording views of people and landscapes. These murals depict scenes of burgeoning industrialism against a pastoral backdrop: timber-frame mine headgear framed by mountains and blue gum trees; the bustling platforms of Park Station against a cloudy blue sky; a ship arriving at dusk into East London Harbour as the water reflects the setting sun.

Palmer was particularly interested in African tribal subjects. One of the most striking is a pastoral landscape that centres on two women, one dressing the other's hair into a geometric form. In another, two women in Muslim dress are standing on a riverbank in what might be East Africa, gazing out towards the mail ship.

ADOLF HITLER'S TYPEWRITER

The keys of the Führer

ABSA Money Museum
15 Troye Street
Open: Monday—Friday 8am—4pm
Free entry

"It's like London in here," says the security guard. It's certainly a stark contrast from the buildings across the road: one a discount corner shop, the other a block of low-cost flats with washing drying on the balcony. Take the escalator one floor up inside ABSA's downtown campus and it's like you have entered a parallel world; a multi-storey building of glass and steel that generates nearly all of its own electricity from onsite gas turbines.

The real surprise is in the money museum. For the most part, it's as you would expect: old customer service counters from the four banks that merged to form ABSA (Volkskas, Allied, United and Trust Bank), a vast collection of quirky old money boxes, calculator machines and the most complete collection of old South African money in the world.

"Old money is like old art. It's a tradable commodity. If we hadn't collected it, it would have been in private hands," says Paul Bayliss, curator of the Money Museum.

Most fascinating, however, over in the section of old typewriters, is a black Underwood Standard, manufactured in 1930/31, that once belonged to Adolf Hitler, and that he used for private correspondence before he became Chancellor of Germany.

According to the display information, Hitler sold the typewriter to a friend called Joseph Matzner who he knew from when they both lived in Braunau am Inn, on the Austrian-Germany border. Matzner went on to become a confectioner in Mauerkirchen, close to Braunau, before emigrating to South Africa, with the typewriter, in 1936.

But these few facts only serve to wet the appetite: Matzner is a Jewish name, and Hitler only lived in Brauanu until he was three years old. The family then moved 50 kilometres away to Passau in Germany, and later to Austria. How was it that Hitler had a Jewish friend who he kept in touch with, even when their lives took them in separate directions?

In South Africa, Matzner's daughter later married a Mr. R. Mauff. When Mauff died, the typewriter was purchased by the Volkskas Bank Museum.

Naturally, Volkskas's decision to acquire this piece of history will certainly raise some eyebrows. During the apartheid years, Volkskas was the main Afrikaner bank, and in the lead up to World War One, many far-right Afrikaners, including those who went on to join the now defunct far-right political party AWB, were vehemently against South Africa joining the war on the side of the Allied powers. They had wanted to fight for Hitler instead.

ST. MARY'S THE LESS CHURCH ㉙

The city's oldest place of worship

41 Park Street
Jeppestown
Open: Services every Sunday at 9:30 am;
special services are posted on the notice board
Tel: 011-614-9029

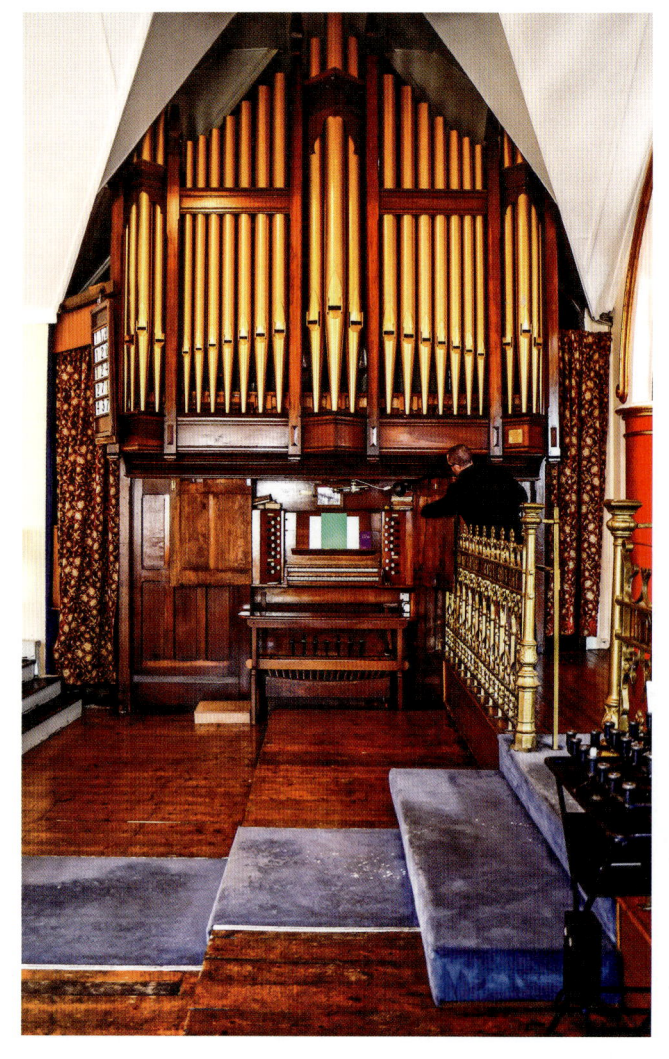

Despite its subservient title, St. Mary's the Less maintains a quiet dignity among the bustle of Jeppestown's chop shops, light industrial businesses and residential semis.

The demure little church was built in 1889, three years after gold was discovered, and is the city's oldest place of worship. It's also quite possibly Jo'burg's oldest surviving building. The quaint red tin roof and whitewashed exterior enclose a gentle incense-scented interior with wooden floors, sky blue and white walls and elegant stained glass windows.

If you look down the length of the church towards the pulpit, you'll notice the wall on the street side leans out considerably. Perhaps due to a mine-related tremor, or more likely down to poor building expertise in Johannesburg in the 1800s.

If you sift through the church's items chronologically, a mini history of Johannesburg unfolds. The pipe organ bought from the British firm Morgan and Smith in 1908 still bellows out hymns every Sunday. Even the church bell has a story behind it.

The original bell lies in the depths of the Atlantic. During World War One, it had been recast and was on its return voyage when the ship carrying it was blown up by a German torpedo. The "new" bell is inscribed with the legend, "St. Mary's Jeppestown. Recast 1917. Sunk on Alnwick Castle 19 March 1917. Replaced by insurance January 1918."

The serene white statue of Mary also has a story. She was donated by congregants in 1918 in memory of sub-deacon Albert Lee, who died in the flu epidemic that swept through Jo'burg that year.

And then there is the stately leather-bound church bible, which bears inscriptions of births and marriages dating as far back as 1841, prior to the building of the church.

Half a shul

The remains of another original place of worship can be found nearby on the corner of Janie and Marshall Streets at the Stonhenge, a marble, granite factory.

At the back of the property is a double-storey, red brick building that tapers to a strange triangular angle. The Lithuanian Synagogue was built in 1903 to serve a burgeoning Jewish population, and was once the gem of the Jewish community in Jeppestown. When it was built, the 400-seat synagogue was adequate to serve the small suburban community, but by 1926 a larger, grander, synagogue took its place. The original synagogue was sold in 1928, and to add insult to injury it was cut in half from corner to corner to make way for the railway expansion, leaving the "half a shul" that remains today.

SALISBURY HOUSE

A Victorian fridge at a school of philosophy

The School of Practical Philosophy
420 Marshall Street
Belgravia
Tel: 0861-66-6688
www.practicalphilosophy.org.za

The pavement outside of the School of Practical Philosophy (otherwise known as Salisbury House) in Belgravia features an interesting checkerboard of sandblasted glass in faded colours. The grid-like structure, which is repeated a few times along the sidewalk, appears to serve some kind of decorative function, or perhaps as a lid concealing a drain or municipal underground passage. These kinds of grids used to be fairly common in the older parts of Jo'burg, usually situated outside old-school corner cafés, but are now mostly relegated to memory.

For those in the know, however, the glass offers a hint to the building's Victorian past when it was a row of early shop houses. Built in 1903, Salisbury House initially had no electricity, and the colourful grids formed part of a primitive refrigeration system. If you venture downstairs into the cool basement of the building, you'll see that the pieces of glass extend into triangular prisms below the surface of the sidewalk.

The basement rooms were used as cool rooms for fresh foodstuffs, while the shards would reflect light into the rooms, without allowing heat in, so that traders could see what was going on. Amazingly the majority of the prisms at Salisbury house are still in place, with only a few of the squares patched in with wood.

The historic building suffered vandalism and stood in a state of neglect for a number of years before being restored to its Victorian glory. The basement rooms now serve as a mini museum and store rooms for bicycles and cleaning equipment, while the rest of the house has been beautifully transformed into classrooms and lecture halls.

The School of Practical Philosophy — which offers courses in, among other things, philosophy and meditation — approached the Johannesburg Property Company (which owned the building) at the turn of the millennium with the offer of restoring Salisbury House. It took another five years to carefully patch and polish it back into shape, while conserving as many of the original features as possible. These include the original wood and glass apothecary cabinets that stand in the portion of the building that once belonged to Anderson's Chemist but is now used as a main lecture hall. A piece of the original wallpaper is protected behind a pane of glass.

Interestingly, Salisbury House stands on the border of Belgravia at the point where it meets Jeppestown. Although there is not much to distinguish the ramshackle suburbs these days, Jeppestown in the early 1900s was seen as working class, while Belgravia was considered to be more upmarket. To mark the distinction (and pay for the maintenance of the road into Belgravia), Johannesburg's very first toll road was erected on the corner of Berg and Marshall Streets across from Salisbury. It proved extremely unpopular and was dismantled shortly thereafter.

VESTIGES OF A TRAM STATION

A takeaway in a tram station

458 Jules Avenue
Malvern

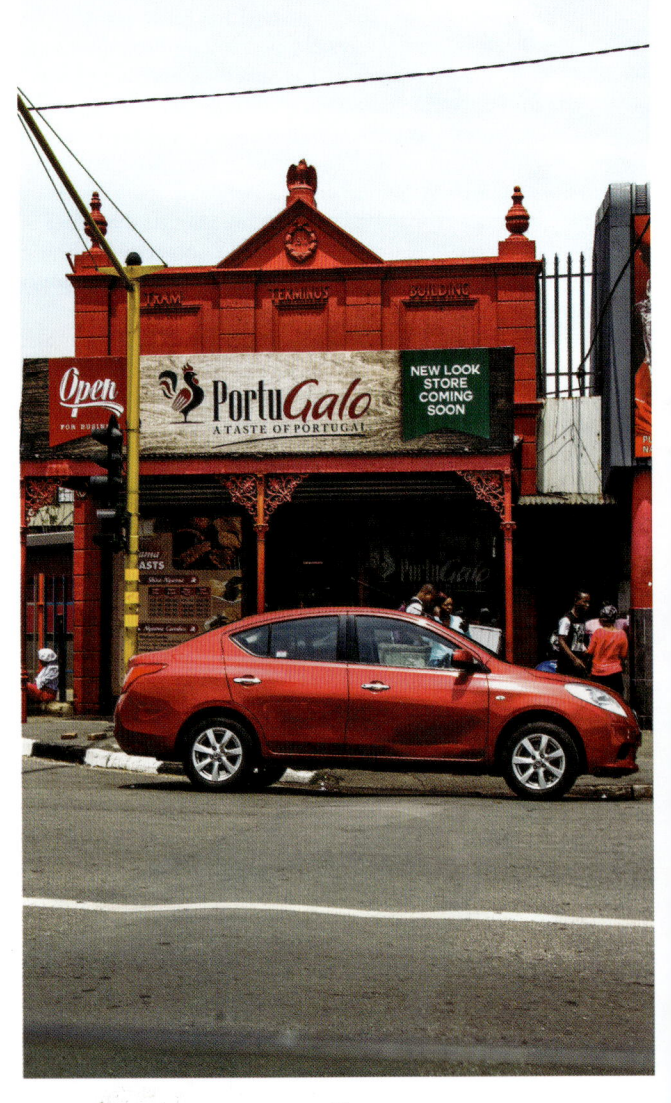

If you ignore the hot scent of burning brakes at number 458 and close your eyes, the jostling of Jules Street can almost take you back to the early days of transport in Johannesburg, when feet, bicycles and electric trams clanked their way from the city to the newly built suburbs on its outskirts.

The energy outside on busy Jules Street is equally frenetic, with double parked trucks and taxis hooting and tearing down the strip at a terrifying pace. Jules is the longest, straightest street in Johannesburg, lined by panelbeaters, semi-detached houses, and the long-standing Mediterranean Fish Centre. It's also one of the original byways from the city to Malvern, which was optimistically named after the tranquil spa town in England, supposedly because it offered a gentle retreat from the bedlam of early Johannesburg's city centre.

It's to Jules Street that the 458 owes its origins. The building is currently a Portuguese takeaway, clad in cheerful posters offering chicken and prawns, shisa nyama, burgers and pap and gravy. But it has also served as a bakery, an electrical depot and a hardware store. The quaint red building began its life as a tram depot station — a vital part of the early public transport system of the city.

According to the book *Johannesburg Tramways* by Tony Spit, "The track was single and laid out in the centre of the gravel road, the overhead being hung from span wires ... The Malvern route distinguished itself by being the longest stretch of straight track in Johannesburg, almost three miles along Jules Street. At the Monmouth Street Terminus, a small depot and quarters for staff were constructed to house the last two outward cars of the day, which returned first thing in the morning as the first two city bound cars ... It was a flourishing route from the beginning and always carried a frequent service."

Malvern might not be the peaceful oasis it was once touted as, but for tram aficionados it offers a place to tune out the blaring of traffic and the whistling of taxi touts, while contemplating a quieter, calmer time in Johannesburg's transport history.

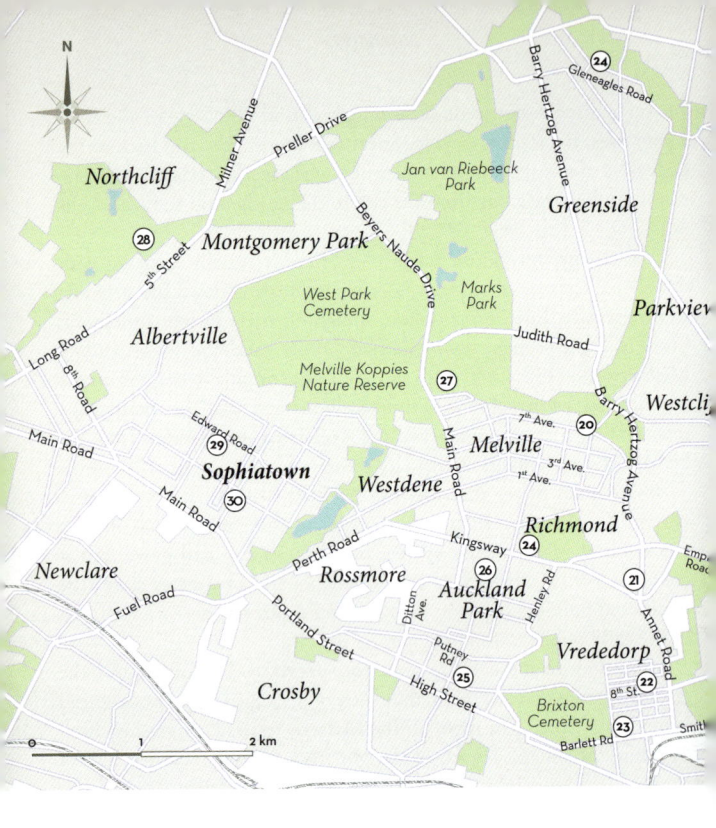

Sophiatown, The Parks, Houghton

①	BALDINELLI'S MOSAIC OF JESUS	78
②	SONS OF ENGLAND CROSS	80
③	HOUGHTON WATERFALL	82
④	MINIATURE RAILWAY OF OBSERVATORY	84
⑤	MAGNETIC ROCKS OF OBS	86
⑥	YUKON'S MISSING WINDOWS	88
⑦	YEOVILLE'S FESTIVAL BELLS	90
⑧	HERMAN CHARLES BOSMAN IN JOHANNESBURG	92
⑨	BAMBANANI URBAN GARDEN	94
⑩	TROYEVILLE'S "BEDTIME STORY"	96
⑪	SCULPTURES IN AN OVERGROWN LOT	98
⑫	HIGHLANDS ROAD SCOTTISH VESTIGES	100
⑬	DAVID WEBSTER HOUSE	102
⑭	BYZANTINE PLUMBER'S YARD	104
⑮	MR. TRILETY'S NOSE SHAPER	106
⑯	THE SPRINGBOK OF THE REGIMENTAL HQ OF THE TRANSVAAL SCOTTISH	108
⑰	VILLA ARCADIA	110

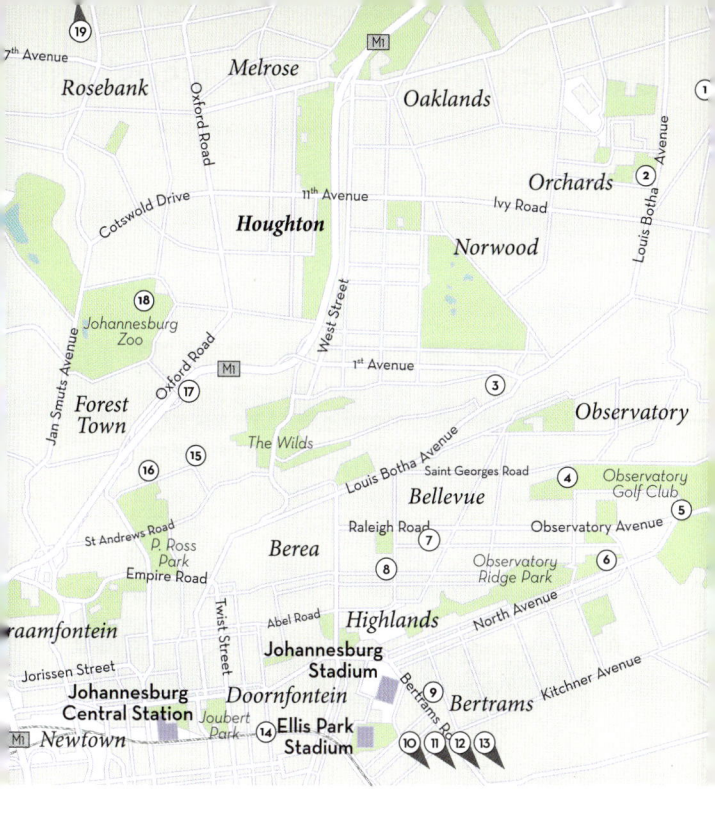

⑱	THE MESSERSCHMITT 262 JET NIGHT FIGHTER	112
⑲	HYDE PARK SHOPPING CENTRE ART COLLECTION	114
⑳	MELVILLE WATERFALL	116
㉑	HISTORIC FRENCH PRESS IN "THE ATELIER"	118
㉒	LAM RIM TIBETAN BUDDHIST CENTRE	120
㉓	FIETAS MUSEUM	122
㉔	CHAMPION TREES	124
㉕	CHURCH OF ST. NICHOLAS OF JAPAN	126
㉖	LINDFIELD VICTORIAN HOUSE MUSEUM	128
㉗	THE PARANOID TREE	130
㉘	GAUTENG'S ARTESIAN SPRING	132
㉙	TREVOR HUDDLESTON'S CENOTAPH	134
㉚	SOPHIATOWN'S HERITAGE TREE	136

BALDINELLI'S MOSAIC OF JESUS ①

A religious creation by one of South Africa's most famous artists

Our Lady of the Wayside
9 St. Mary's Road
Maryvale
Open: Daily 8am—5pm

Residents of Maryvale will probably have noticed the mosaic façade of Maryvale Parish church. But unless you are parishioner, you will probably never have seen the giant mosaic of the crucifixion of Jesus Christ that stretches up to the church roof behind the altar.

Commissioned in the 1950s by James Droste, a steel merchant and benefactor to the church, the mosaic was made by one of South Africa's most famous artists from the latter part of last century, Armando Baldinelli.

Baldinelli, along with Edoardo Villa and Giuseppe Cattaneo, belonged to a notable group of Italian artists who moved to South Africa during and after World War Two.

"There was a strong Italian contingent in the art world," explains Karel Nel, artist and associate professor of art at Wits University.

Born in 1908 in Ancona, a seaport in central Italy, the young Baldinelli studied classical art in Bologna, Rome and Modena, before going on to make a special study of the early Byzantine mosaics and frescoes of Ravenna. In 1933, he exhibited at the Venice Biennale, which is still to this day one of the most prestigious events on the global art calendar.

Like many Europeans after the war, Baldinelli came to South Africa in search of a better life. During the 1950s, food was still being rationed in Europe and life was hard.

From his classical buildings in South Africa, Baldinelli began experimenting with what he called "stone paintings" – complex mosaics that included shells, glass and stones, as well as the usual tesserae.

"His skill was excellent. His tesserae are chipped in a regular manner and very beautifully laid," says Nel.

Baldinelli's works were often commissioned for public spaces, and although many of them have disappeared, two still remain: one outside the cinema toilets at Hyde Park Shopping centre (see p.118), and this towering mosaic at Our Lady of the Wayside.

Baldinelli was a devout Catholic. This was his parish church, and one can only imagine he must have taken great pleasure in creating art linked to his faith.

Rather fittingly, when Baldinelli died in 2002, a requiem mass in his honour was held in the church.

SONS OF ENGLAND CROSS

A cross saved from the ashes

Orchards Project
Orchards
Open: By appointment only
Tel: 011-622-8297

The battle of the Somme was one of the bloodiest in human history. Fought on French soil during World War One, more than one million men were wounded or killed, including those of the 3rd infantry of the Transvaal Regiment, who fell in October 1916.

To commemorate the fallen soldiers, a giant cross was carved from an oak tree from the actual battlefield. The cross was installed first in the garden of the Sons of England club in Orange Grove, and later in Paterson Park, a popular recreational park for white, blue-collar families during apartheid.

The pressures of post-apartheid South Africa saw the park fall into neglect, and in 2012, the cross found itself face to face with a common South African enemy — poverty. To keep warm on a winter's night, vagrants had wrenched the cross from the memorial and thrown it onto a fire.

Fortunately, serendipity intervened when Zoleka Mtobeni, a citizen with links to the Joburg Heritage Foundation, happened to be walking by and saw the cross being burned. Quick intervention saved the cross from destruction and it was taken for safekeeping to the nearby Orchards Project, an arts and skills development centre close to the park.

"Nothing is sacred anymore," says Roger Chadwick with a heavy heart, propping the slightly charred cross against the wall inside the Orchards studio.

It is an issue worthy of debate. As the saying goes, one man's rubbish is another man's treasure. And the converse is also true. In a contested city, its identity continually in flux, is it fair to expect one man's treasure to be respected and valued by another?

Of course, it is South Africa's highest hope that we will begin to truly value our diversity, that we will begin to listen to and care about histories that are not our own, but from which we can still learn valuable insights about the human condition and our place in the world. But first, everybody needs to eat. Jo'burg is a city with vast gaps between the rich and the poor, the haves and the have nots. Perhaps we are not there yet.

HOUGHTON WATERFALL

③

A forgotten watering hole

Corner of Louis Botha Avenue and Houghton Drive
Open: Access via Police Reservists Training Centre (ask permission)

With taxis hurtling down from Hillbrow towards "Death Bend", Louis Botha Avenue is the last place on earth you would expect to find a waterfall. In recent years, constant roadworks, as the city endeavours to bring the Rea Vaya public bus system to this busy thoroughfare, have turned the avenue into a corridor of chaos. But tucked away behind the graffiti walls, close to a plaque commemorating the site of a British blockhouse built during the Anglo-Boer War, is a four metre cascade.

The best way to access the waterfall is to knock on the door of the Police Reservists Training Centre on the corner of Houghton Drive and ask permission to access their back garden. They lease the land from the City. Pick your way through the overgrown garden, keeping right to avoid wet feet, and find the best route through the thick grasses, thorny bushes and unfortunate rubbish. Within a minute or so, the waterfall appears.

The source of the water is the north-flowing Sandspruit, which bubbles up out of the ground in Bellevue East — giving the appearance more of a burst pipe than a natural stream. The water flows under Louis Botha then drops through two pools, before cascading another four metres down rocks to a larger pool.

The sound of the falling water is not really loud enough to drown out the traffic on Louis Botha, but there is something charming about standing there; a gentle reminder of a time not all that long ago, before gold was discovered, when this was farm land, and this waterfall would have brought pleasure and sustenance to the people and animals who spent their days around this ridge.

From the reservists' garden, the water runs in an open stone channel for about 20 metres, before continuing underground across Houghton Drive, through the Houghton golf course, through Paterson Park, until it appears again and is canalised at the Birdhaven Bird Sanctuary in Melrose. The stream then continues on to Sandton, joining the Braamfontein Spruit at Sunninghill Park, before finally completing its urban meander at the Jukskei River.

MINIATURE RAILWAY OF OBSERVATORY

The Rattlesnake River and Bear Mountain Railroad

Observatory Driving Range
5 Steyn Street
Open: Saturday 11am—3pm by appointment only
Tel: Clive 011-974-7425

In a dull brick building with slit windows at the far end of the Observatory Driving Range is a tiny world that will take your breath away.

Mountains made of sculpted polystyrene, rivers and waterfalls made from PratliGlo, logging factories, train stations, bridges, gold mining towns, and a lighthouse in a turbulent sea. Snaking between it all, a railway track, everything painstakingly hand crafted by the members of the Rand Model Railway Club.

The club has been going since 1946, a hobby that arrived in South Africa with the British immigrants who came post-World War Two.

"It was the sort of recreation that a non-sporting dad would do to spend time with his land," says club chairman, Clive Shepherd.

The club's first home was at the agricultural grounds of the Rand Easter Show, but when that land was appropriated for Wits University's West Campus in the early 1980s, the club relocated to this old sports changing room. Back then, Observatory was a predominantly Jewish neighbourhood. Nowadays, when the club meets for their weekly Saturday sessions, the streets are shared between orthodox Jews with their large brethrens, prostitutes, and boy racers, who like revving their fast cars around the hilly roads.

"It's a most surreal situation," says Shepherd of his medley of neighbours. "But once you're inside here, you don't care what happens out there."

The eight club members are mostly in their sixties, except for Gareth Knowles, an IT specialist by profession, who inspired the older guys to get rid of the railway's old British and German toy towns, and create, from scratch, an American mountain wonderland.

That said, British locomotives still ride these lines, including a miniature replica of the Black Five, the 1945 steam locomotive that transported British soldiers back to their homes in England and Scotland after World War Two — its magic enhanced by the 'choo-choo' sound effects and the squeal of brakes when it pulls in to stations. Other trains in the collection include a replica of the Orient Express and the train on which Hitler made the French sign their surrender.

Olivia Menhinick, the co-owner of the Observatory Driving Range, who had been on site for six years, had no idea that it was there. "This is absolutely amazing," she said, entering the shed for the first time. "We normally take the kids to Knysna to see something like this. You don't expect to see this kind of thing in Jo'burg."

MAGNETIC ROCKS OF OBS

⑤

The geological remains of an inland sea

Observatory Golf Course
5 Steyn Street
Open: Monday, by appointment only
Tel: 011-648-9579

Ever wonder why Jo'burg has such a strong pull over you? The answer can be found in the corner of the Observatory Golf Course.

Just a few blocks away from the vibrant, buzzing streets of Yeoville, now home to a large immigrant Congolese population, is the Observatory golf course — possibly one of the most serene and beautiful valleys in all of Johannesburg.

Originally built in 1914 on an old refuse dump, the place has evolved over the last century into a green lung for the city, peppered with pine and birch trees, and a large flock of Indian myna birds. Its golfing claim to fame is that it was the club of Bobby Locke, four-time winner of the Open Championship (UK) and nine South African Opens. However, it also has a link to Jo'burg's biggest trophy — gold.

Next to the 15th tee box is a patch of exposed jagged red and black rocks. Fish a coin out of your pocket and play about with it on the rocks. You will notice that there are places where the magnetic pull is so strong, the coin sticks.

Writing in his book, *Historic Overview of the Witwatersrand Goldfields*, J.R.F. Handley explains that during the years 1925 to 1933, people were beginning to predict that the goldfields were exhausted. Things took a turn in the 1930s when Dr. Rudolf Krahmann, a German-trained geophysicist, arrived in South Africa.

While attending a motor racing event at Muldersdrift (where gold had already been discovered) Krahmann noted that magnetic crystals were present on the shale on which he was sitting. Krahmann reasoned that if he could map the position of the magnetic shale, it would be possible to calculate the position of the main gold reef and thus narrow down the ground that had to be prospected for drilling.

His idea worked. With pinpoint accuracy his magnetometer surveys led to the opening up of the West Wits Line, one of the richest gold fields in South Africa, and to the discovery of the Evander, Klerksdorp and Free State gold fields.

The rock on the Observatory course, which consists of thin layers of black magnetic shale alternating with white layers of siliceous rock called chert, also points to the fact that this area was once an inland sea — such high levels of iron and silica are normally only found in sea water.

YUKON'S MISSING WINDOWS ⑥

A low-key yet unique place to host events

Yukon House
33 North Avenue
Bezuidenhout Valley
Open: By appointment with Loretta Morris Chamberlain
Tel: 072-025-9164

It is normally Parktown that is associated with Randlord mansions, relics of the gold and diamond mining boom. But there is another grand old dame in Bez Valley.

Yukon House, named after the region in Canada where its first owner, Tommy Allen, made his fortune in diamonds and gold, is the private home of Loretta Morris Chamberlain, who loves to share it with those looking for a low-key yet unique place to host events. The building has a fascinating history.

Allen, who became one of the first mayors of Johannesburg, commissioned it to be built in the style of a Masonic Lodge (he was a member).

The Corinthian painting stained glass windows in his billiards room were acquired from the London Stock Exchange, which was undergoing refurbishment, and the walls were panelled with wood from the Afrimosa tree — now extinct.

Allen lived here until 1929, when he lost all of his fortune in the stock market crash. The building then went through many incarnations, including a boys hostel in the 1940s, and a Centre for Christian Spirituality.

"We'd been looking for an old house and we felt an instant connection when we walked in," says Chamberlain, pointing out the Carrera marble floors and an art nouveau fireplace. She has turned the former billiards room, with its sprung floor, into a wedding chapel.

The terraced gardens are as enchanting as the interiors, especially when their pet Indian peacock, Dali, is strutting his stuff. He is not always to be seen though. Dali has a habit of going AWOL: on one of his more recent escapades he found his way to a nearby Indian family's home and refused to come back for a month.

Another thing that has gone missing are the stained glass windows. In the 1980s, Mr. Avlonitis, the then owner, acquired funding from the Heritage Foundation to restore the windows but instead sold them on the sly to someone in the UK. There is one window remaining, however, halfway up the hand-carved wooden staircase, though you might not want to linger too long on the stairs.

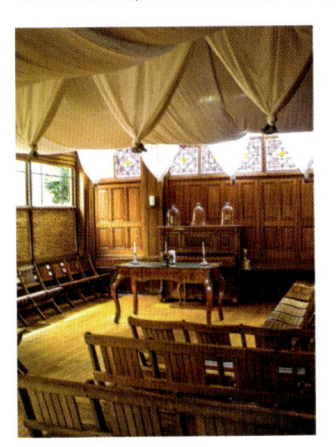

"We have two ghosts," says Chamberlain, who comes from a family of clairvoyants. "Two naughty little boys. They are always hiding things."

Perhaps getting rid of the windows was their idea.

YEOVILLE'S FESTIVAL BELLS ⑦

Belgian bells in an Afrocentric suburb

St. Aidan's Anglican Church
59 Regent Street
Yeoville
Transport: Catch a minibus taxi to the rank on 81 Raleigh Street. From there it is a 400m walk to the church. Turn left from the taxi rank, immediately right into Bedford Road and take the third right onto Regent Street.
Open: Monday—Thursday 9am—3pm. Sunday services are at 7:30am and 9:30am and at 8:30am on every last Sunday of the month

Where most suburbs fall into a sleepy lull come Sunday, the streets of Yeoville come alive with the fashionistas of the Sunday service circuit. Brightly clad worshippers of all denominations spill out onto the streets where they meet and greet and make plans for the remains of their weekend. Zionists walk the street in white robes and outside the walls of St Aidan's Anglican Church, women in African wax-print dresses carry dolled-up babies and clutch the hands of small boys wearing shiny shoes and tiny suits exactly like their fathers'.

Yeoville has traditionally been a starting point for migrants to the city, so much so that it's referred to colloquially as Hotel Yeoville, because immigrants who face discrimination and xenophobia in other parts of the city feel welcome here. In the gold-rush era, the area saw an influx of Eastern European Jews. By the 1970s and 1980s, it was a popular bohemian hangout for politically aware artists and writers. But in recent years the demographic has changed to micro-communities from African countries such as Nigeria, Democratic Republic of Congo, Ethiopia, Somalia, Ghana, Ivory Coast, Mozambique, Zimbabwe and other parts of the continent.

St. Aidan's was established in 1912 to serve an Anglican Christian denomination and has a healthy congregation to this day. The nave was extended in 1922 and the building was finally completed in 1937. If you dare to venture up a set of stairs and a perilous series of iron rungs and claw your way up into the very top of the belfry, you'll find a series of cast iron bells of varying sizes. The bells are distinctive in that they are played by means of an electric piano one floor below. They are one of only four sets of carillon bells in South Africa.

Typically, a carillon is composed of at least 23 bells of different sizes and tonalities that are tuned to create a harmony when played together. The bells are currently dormant as they are badly in need of expensive specialist servicing.

They were imported by a festival committee in 1961 and were intended be used in a celebration of Johannesburg's 75th birthday. However, it wasn't a terribly well thought through plan because once the bells arrived, the committee realised they had no place to put them. The "temporary" solution was to house them at the Anglican Church where they remain to this day. Heritage aficionados are attempting to find funding to restore the bells to their festival glory.

HERMAN CHARLES BOSMAN IN JOHANNESBURG

A wild, bohemian lifestyle stranger than fiction

Murder site: 19 Isipingo Street, Bellevue East
Grave site: Plot number 3942, West Park Cemetery

Popular author Herman Charles Bosman was best known for his Voorkamer Stories — dry, ironic yarns told by protagonist Oom Schalk Lourens — which brought the unique characters and stories of the small town farming district of Marico to life. In fact, if you visit Groot Marico in the North West province, you'll find a number of long-bearded, pipe smoking Oom Schalk Lourens lookalikes, not to mention a Herman Charles Bosman Literary Society and regular themed Bosman festivals and weekends.

The author is so revered in that part of the world that it might be surprising to realise that he spent only one year of his life as a teacher in Marico. He did most of his writing (and living) in Johannesburg, where his wild, bohemian lifestyle lived up to the adage "stranger than fiction".

Biographers offer disparate accounts of the author's life that paint him variously as a gentle genius or an outright monster. According to legend, Bosman ran a postal order scam in his teenage years and at one point, while living in London, faked his death to elicit funeral money from his mother. He's said to have performed a number of abortions, including one on his third wife. Then there is the small matter of murder.

A blue heritage plaque marks the Bellevue East house where Bosman shot dead his stepbrother David Russel on 18 July 1929. The story goes that the two got into an argument and Bosman shot Russel with a hunting rifle. Sentenced to death row, he got a massive reprieve and ended up serving only four and a half years. Some sources claim the shooting was an accident, others that it was a fit of mania.

He was only 46 when he died of heart failure in 1951, most likely preempted by considerable financial stress and a propensity for drinking vast amounts of Coca Cola. But the stories didn't stop there. They continued to follow Bosman beyond the grave when one of the author's greatest fans sought permission to be buried beside him.

It's not clear why Bosman was buried in a double site, but when the actor Patrick Mynhardt found out, he decided that the author would be a good companion in the afterlife. Mynhardt, himself a great storyteller, had attained a measure of fame through his series of one-man shows portraying Herman Charles Bosman's time in prison and on death row.

The actor would load up his beige Mazda and Venter trailer to tour South Africa's small towns where his shows became increasingly popular. So it was apt that his last wish was for his coffin to be loaded on to the Venter and towed to his final resting place by his old Mazda.

And so it is that two great storytellers continue to spin wild yarns into eternity.

BAMBANANI URBAN GARDEN ⑨

An organic market garden on an old bowling green

46 Bertrams Road
Open: Every day 9am—5pm

Jo'burg is a city in transition, and few places epitomise this flux more than the Bambanani Urban Garden in the suburb of Bertrams. Before 1994, this land — across the road from Ellis Park Stadium and overlooked by the Ponte City skyscraper — was a whites-only bowling green and recreation club.

A heady cocktail of white fear and a spike in violent crime saw this neighbourhood abandoned by those who could afford to go elsewhere. By the early 2000s, the bowling green had become an unofficial dumping ground for the new residents of Bertrams, many of them living close to the breadline.

All that began to change in 2007 when Amon Maluleke, a security guard from the neighbouring cricket club, had the idea of turning this abandoned land into a vegetable garden. Originally a subsistence farmer from rural Limpopo, Amon, like many young men, had left the farm to seek his fortune in the big city.

"The very thing he was running away from followed him to Jo'burg," laughs Amon's brother Ronnie, who is now one of the eight Bambanani urban farmers. Bambanani means "we hold each other together".

"I'm so proud of my brother. Agriculture is in his blood and it's also in mine. I've realised that I belong to the soil. My big house is in this soil. My car is in this soil. I have to dig this soil. This is my treasure."

Another member of the team, Zeb Molefe, agrees. But he admits that many of the local youth think they are mad. "You can see them thinking, 'Are those guys slaves?' But we can't all be modern and work in an office. Someone has to feed us. We can't forget our roots. Everything comes from the land. Without land you have nothing."

They lease the land from the City of Joburg. Across four polytunnels and an open field, the team grow spinach, aubergine, carrots, kale, peppers, maize, sweet potatoes, gem squash, and a selection of herbs. Everything is organic. They don't use any pesticides, instead choosing to intercrop, planting sweet basil next to lettuce to keep away the slugs and attract the bees.

From Thursday to Saturday they welcome shoppers from the local community, and anyone else passing by who wants to buy vegetables at prices much lower than the supermarkets. Bambanani works as a cooperative, and at the end of the year, they share the profits.

TROYEVILLE'S "BEDTIME STORY" ⑩

A concrete bed on a roadside

Corner of Albertina Sisulu and Viljoen Streets
Troyeville

A strange sight greets anyone passing by the grassy corner of Albertina Sisulu and Viljoen Streets in Troyeville. A bed with an impressive, plushly quilted headboard, draped with white, silky sheets and pillows lies as if waiting for Sleeping Beauty or some other mystery slumberer to return to its folds.

On closer inspection, it's not some old bed left on the pavement to rot, or to be reclaimed by a student or homeless person, but a cleverly crafted cement slab with concrete sheeting that mimics the drapery of an unmade bed.

The bed has an unusual back story. Installed on the corner in 2011, it was the brainchild of the late public art consultant Lesley Perkes. Perkes reportedly drove past the corner almost daily on her route to drop her children at school. At that time, there was a pile of facebrick rubble on the site, so Perkes decided to take matters into her own hands and replace the eyesore with something quirky and creative.

She approached artist and photographer Johannes Dreyer. Together they came up with the concept of a bed as a place for dreams to be realised. Dreyer in turn approached designer Damien Grivas and they modelled the bed from a cheap headboard they picked up in Primrose.

The original post from Perkes blog reads, "The truth is, even when it wasn't rubble, the irredeemable yellow facebrick (my worst) object made no sense: It was just an inexplicable platform with an equally inexplicable thing on top of it; of no apparent use and never good to look at it.

"Local hitman Johannes Dreyer is conspiring with concrete form worker Damien Grivas of Bez Valley to ensure the view will, at the very least, soon become more interesting. In pursuit of their plan, #lesmiserables and the hitman spent some rainy afternoon time in Primrose this week sourcing a suitably kitsch headboard. Found for R450.00 in the first second-hand shop on the right. Watch this public space."

For a number of years the bed was used as a site to hold poetry readings, pyjama parties with bedtime stories, and art installations; it was even yarn bombed once. All of which was recorded on a blog maintained by Perkes.

The artist sadly passed away in 2015 after a long battle with cancer, but Troyeville's Bedtime Story remains on the corner where it will continue to serve as a play space for children and to provoke curiosity and imagination among passers-by.

SCULPTURES
IN AN OVERGROWN LOT

⑪

Angels of Troyeville

Spaza Art Gallery
19 Wilhemina Street
Troyeville

With a reputation as crime-riddled as Johannesburg's, it's hardly surprising that the majority of the city's oldest remaining buildings are churches, synagogues and other religious institutions. If ever there was a city in need of salvation, this is it. So the presence of a number of winged concrete statues looming from the long grass of what appears to be a vacant lot, like angelic apparitions in the heart of Troyeville's suburbia, is really rather comforting.

For passers by the angels seem to have appeared on the lot through some kind of divine intervention — sent to watch over the city's silhouette from behind rusty wire fencing. Their broad frames are solid and friendly and stand as non-judgemental protectors for all, regardless of religious belief.

Anyone familiar with the chubby, white-robed "Angel of the North" (standing like an African version of Brazil's "Christ the Redeemer" with arms widespread at the corner of Queens and Kotze Streets, opposite the Constitutional Court in Hillbrow), will immediately recognise the angels as the work of informal artist Winston Luthuli.

Luthuli was born and raised in KwaZulu-Natal but moved to Johannesburg on 1989. The artist has a number of angels dotted around public spaces in Jozi and Soweto. However, he insists his angels are not representative of Christianity alone, rather they act as symbols in the folklore of many religions and can be viewed simply as higher beings.

The lot is in fact Luthuli's outdoor workshop and a part of the Spaza Art Gallery, an NGO and community exhibition space that also hosts workshops, poetry readings, comedy shows and live music. It was started in 2001 by artist Andrew Lindsay, who grew tired of being a landlord and decided instead to turn his property into a quirky community space with the aim of showcasing work by artists from across South Africa. Lindsay had been working in creating public arts and met a number of artists who were battling to break into the industry. The idea behind Spaza was to create a friendly place where emerging artists, buyers and appreciators could meet and mingle.

The works in the lot are cast-offs, works in progress, or simply angels that haven't found a permanent home yet. In the interim they stand like sentinels guarding the wellbeing of this thriving creative community.

HIGHLANDS ROAD SCOTTISH VESTIGES

A small piece of Scottish suburbia

Between Kensington and Troyeville
Johannesburg

It might have lost its broad brogue over the years, but Highlands Road, connecting the suburbs of Troyeville and Kensington, is an interesting byway filled with Scottish history and nostalgia.

Aside from being a particularly pleasant road to drive along in late spring and early summer when the jacarandas are in purple bloom, Highlands Road is home to a small piece of "forever Scotland".

In 1905, a large Celtic cross was erected on Caledonia hill, at the Kensington end of the road, to commemorate the war efforts of The Scottish Horse. The regiment was raised on the request of Lord Milner, who needed help fighting against the Boers in the First South African War (1899 to 1902). A number of Scots lost their lives in that fight. Incidentally, the regiment was the precursor to the Transvaal Scottish Regiment, which fought in both world wars.

One of Johannesburg's earliest war memorials, the cross overlooks an area that at one point served as one of the largest remount camps in the Anglo Boer War. In 1937, to signify the national pride felt by the Scottish in South Africa, a commemoration was held at the site of the cross.

Mr. A.J. MacDonald, Chief of the Caledonian Society, rather romantically extoled, "I would appeal to all Scotsmen to make this the mecca of an annual pilgrimage, where they can meet under the canopy of heaven on a St. Andrews Sunday afternoon. It is my sincere hope that steps will be taken in the near future to render this one of the beauty spots of the city, for what finer site for this Scottish Monument could have been chosen than this magnificent view site, mountainous and wild, recalling the rugged grandeur of Scotland itself."

A further nod to the Scottish motherland is the Kensington Castle (at 127 Highlands Road), whose stone towers peek above the suburban architecture of the area. The castle is one of only four in Johannesburg, but is probably the most authentic, having allegedly been modelled on Rothesay Castle in Scotland. It was built by Samuel Scott Wilson, who was inspired to bring a piece of Scotland to Johannesburg in 1911 when the woman he fell in love with agreed to marry him on condition that he build her a castle.

Sadly, the couple only lived there for a few years before falling on hard times but they didn't leave without a fight. According to a 2013 article in the *Mail & Guardian*, the couple masqueraded as ghosts, moaning and clanking chains in an attempt to ward off would be buyers.

Highlands Road is also of interest to geologists. It is built on a ridge of raw rock known as diamictite, which comprises fine silt particles with the distinctive inclusion of various type of rocks, such as shale and quartzite. This unusual rock type was probably deposited by mudflows, likely triggered by earthquakes. Similar structures occur at only two other areas associated with the Witwatersrand Supergroup, namely Main Reef and the Kimberley Reef.

DAVID WEBSTER HOUSE

A life's mosaic

13 Eleanor Street
Troyeville

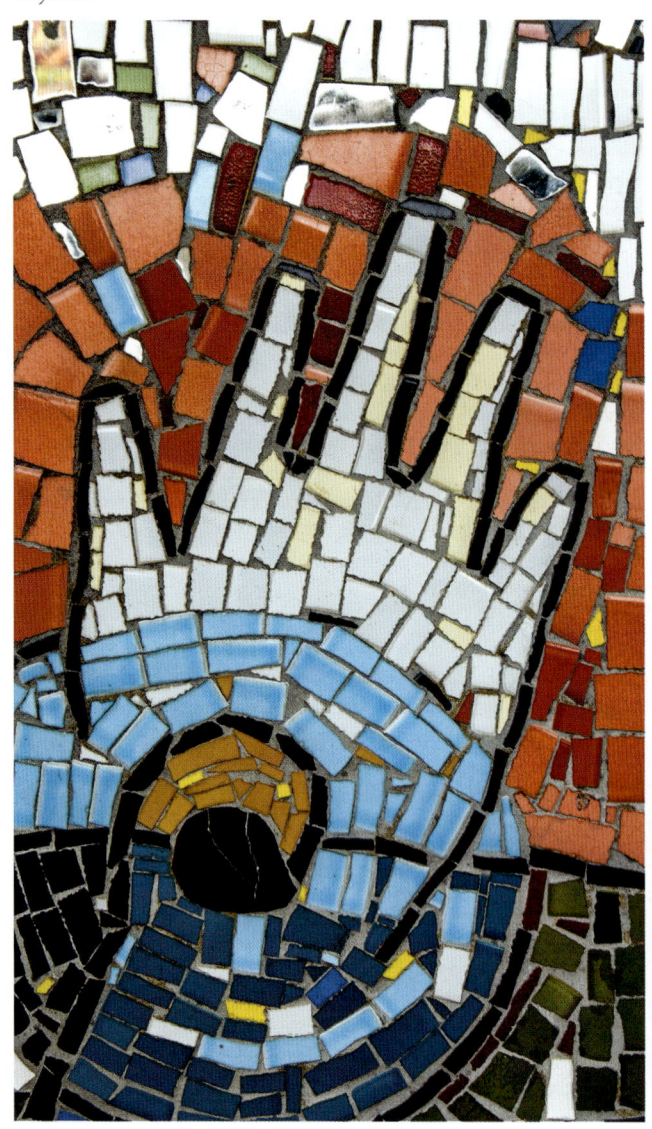

There's a house that stands out on an otherwise unassuming street in the kind of neighbourhood where children still play outdoors. Brightly clad in uplifting mosaics, number 13 Eleanor Street has the aura of an artist's residence. But the cheerful images (flowers and hands, a soccer ball and cattle) belie the brutal story behind the mural.

On 1 May 1989, anti-apartheid activist David Webster was gunned down in the street outside the house, having returned from a walk in the park with his partner Maggie Friedman. Webster was ardent campaigner against detention without trial and was best known for his "tea parties" — gatherings where former detainees and the parents of detainees could meet to swap stories and legal advice. It's this that drew the attention of the ominous security forces.

In his writing, Webster also made a point of highlighting the use of assassination as a means of controlling government opposition, so it is tragically ironic that his life should suffer the same fate. His death, however, was not without consequence. It sparked a barrage of publicity and investigation that ultimately led to the revelation of the existence of a secret death squad in the South African Defence Force known as the Civil Cooperation Bureau.

His assassin, Ferdi Barnard — described by journalist Jaques Pauw as "one of apartheid's most infamous hoodlums, a Rambo-esque killer who moved between the criminal underworld of drug dealing, prostitution and diamond smuggling, and South Africa's official business in the government's dirty tricks units and death squad" — was sentenced in 1999 to two life terms plus 63 years for a number of crimes, including the murder of Webster.

The house was decorated to commemorate 10 years after Webster's death. "We used an image by Paul Klee as a starting point for our inspiration, and included symbols that had personal relevance to David," says Ilsa Pahl, who designed the mosaic in collaboration with Friedman. Members of the close-knit Troyeville community came together to mosaic the walls. "We took actual prints of [their children] Ruby and Leo's hands. There are seeds in various stages of germination to represent growth to show David's connection to the landscape and to people. The sea and Nguni cattle represent his love of the Transkei and cattle are also a symbol of wealth.

"We used a bowl of water as well as open and closed hands as symbols of reconciliation. And the keyhole became our symbol for opening up access to the future." In all, a fitting tribute to a short life, but one that was well lived.

BYZANTINE PLUMBER'S YARD

A forgotten Turkish treasure

Beit Street
Doornfontein
Open: By appointment only
Tel: 083-377-2045

Tucked away inside a plumber's yard in industrial Doornfontein are the remnants of a Byzantine mansion built by Henri "Beetles" Bettelheim, the Turkish consul at the end of the 19th century.

Born of German-Jewish descent in Constantinople, Beetles came to South Africa at the age of 20 and made his money in the diamond markets of Kimberley. He went on to become one of the founders of the Johannesburg Stock Exchange and The Rand Club.

His home, with its Oriental minarets, dome-like stained glass windows and fretted screens, was renown for decadent parties, gambling nights and beautiful women. At one banquet, guest Louis Cohen recalled "the sight of a female form divine being brought in under cover of a dish."

Doornfontein later fell out of favour as a fashionable district as the rich decanted to the leafier suburb of Parktown. And when Ian Lee Fraser, the grandfather of the current owner, bought the property in the 1940s, he turned it into the base for his plumbing business, servicing the many apartment blocks that had sprung up in neighbouring Hillbrow, by then a popular Jewish quarter.

Today, much of the mansion is gone, sacrificed to the utilitarian needs of a plumbing business. But if you look closely, behind stacks of faucets, pipes and toilet bowls, many of the Oriental gems remain.

One room boasts a vaulted ceiling with stars and crescent trim; another ceiling has remnants of a fresco of peacock feathers, while hidden by shelves of nuts and bolts are wooden doors carved with geometrical patterns and richly coloured stained glass windows. But the pièce de résistance must be the surviving brass-domed minaret — the other was destroyed — topped with a rising crescent moon. It makes a curious contrast to the Hillbrow communications tower that rises up behind it.

Since taking over the family business in 2005, plumber Greg Mullins has fallen in love with the building and is slowly beginning to peel back her layers and restore the treasures. His aim is to transform this old gem into a Turkish restaurant. In the meantime, he welcomes fellow romantics to pop by and peer past the pipes to experience this forgotten part of Jo'burg's past.

MR. TRILETY'S NOSE SHAPER ⑮

For the successful correction of ill-shaped noses

Adler Museum of Medicine
Faculty for Health Sciences
7 York Road
Parktown
Open: Monday—Friday 9am—4pm; weekends by appointment.
Tel: 011-717-2081

It is perhaps no surprise in a country with a history of racial profiling like South Africa that there was a time — perhaps there still is — when you would be judged by the shape of your nose. But while noses today get re-engineered with a surgeon's knife, the Adler Medical Museum at Wits University has among its collection a strange contraption that recalls a time when medical innovators hawked their wares direct to the public through catalogues.

Mr. Trilety was a "pioneering nose shaping specialist", originally from Binghamton, New York, later working out of Hatton Garden in London, who claimed that his Trados 25 nose shaper (pictured), when worn daily, was able to reshape hook noses, noses with pronounced bridges, and skew noses — all of which he described as deformities.

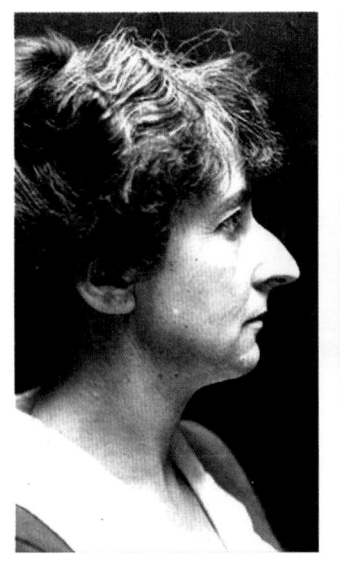

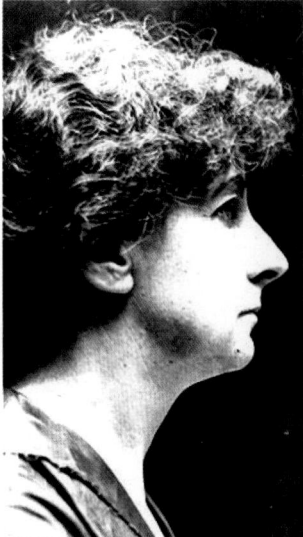

"A Perfect Looking Nose can easily be yours. The Trados 25 corrects now ill-shaped noses quickly, painlessly, permanently and comfortably at home (excepting cases caused by improper bone structure). It is the only adjustable, safe and guaranteed patent device that will actually give you a perfect looking nose. Over 90,000 satisifed users. For years recommended by physicians. Model 25 Junior for children," read one of his many adverts published in magazines around the world.

The Nose Shaper in Adler's collection of medical curiosities is accompanied by a list of 12 undesirable noses, with detailed instructions of which screws to tighten, how much pressure to apply, and which extensions and adjusters to use — "for unusually big, fleshy noses all six adjusters should be used" — in order to achieved the desired effects.

Before applying the nose shaper, patients were instructed to rub the nose with Trilety's "Specially Prepared Massage Cream" to relax the muscles of the nose and supposedly make its reformation easier. He also advised that the device be worn for 30 minutes daily before retiring to bed. Though for even faster results he suggested that "If you sit down to read for 20 or 30 minutes a day, you can wear the appliance without the least inconvenience", cautioning that "to leave off wearing it for a single days until you have obtained a straightened, nicely shaped nose means that you will be obliged to continue the treatment longer than you would have done."

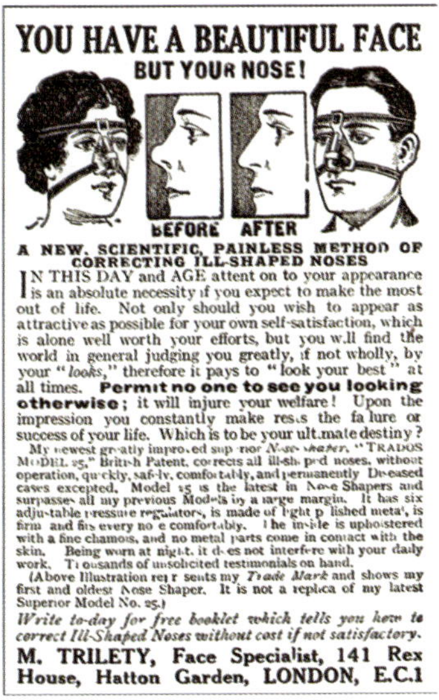

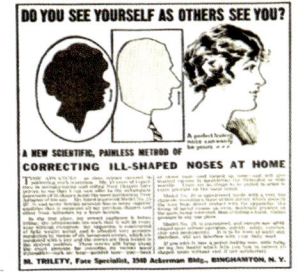

THE SPRINGBOK OF THE REGIMENTAL HQ OF THE TRANSVAAL SCOTTISH

The springbok that went to war

The View
Ridge Road
Parktown
Open: By appointment with regimental historian James Mitchell
Tel: 082-773-2700

Housed in a mansion built by Thomas Cullinan (the chairman of the mine that discovered the world's largest diamond), the regimental headquarters of the Transvaal Scottish, a civilian regiment that has served South Africa since shortly after the South African War, boasts beautiful walls decorated with hand-painted friezes of flowers and birds. Upstairs, it houses a lifelike replica of a little springbok called Nancy — their World War One regimental mascot.

Presented in 1915 by David Maclaren Kennedy, a storekeeper at the Groenfontein colliery in the then Orange Free State, Nancy accompanied the regiment on all their deployments: to Egypt, on a sea passage to Mersa Matruh (where she got sea sick), to the Western Desert (where she went AWOL), and to France, after the campaign against Senussi, where she was much admired in Marseille.

"You don't go to war as a machine. You are doing it for the guy on your left and the guy on your right. It's a family in that sense, and big families do mad things," says regimental historian James Mitchell. "Nancy was their way of saying this is who we are. We are South Africans. She gave them a sense of identity."

Nancy stayed with them in all their battles, eventually suffering a broken horn in the battle in Armentiers in 1917 during the shelling of the transport lines. She died at Hermeton in Belgium on 28 November 1918.

But Nancy's travels didn't end then. Her skin was cured, stuffed in London and sent to Colonel Sir William Dalrymple, the Honorary Colonel of the regiment. For many years she graced the regimental mess, before moving to Ditsong National Museum of Military History. In July 2014, she went travelling again, this time to Scotland with Sandi MacKenzie, Senior Curator of Ditsong National Museum of Military History, to take part in the Common Cause exhibition at the National Museum of Scotland in Edinburgh, which commemorated the lives and stories of soldiers of Scottish descent who served for the Commonwealth nations during the First World War.

Unsurprisingly for itinerant Nancy, she now has two homes in Jo'burg. Her original pelt is at Ditsong while her body double is at The View, which is itself something of a hidden treasure.

The regimental pub serves lunch to the public from Monday to Friday, though there are no signs outside and no menus. You eat whatever the chef has in stock. Springbok burger anyone?

VILLA ARCADIA

⑰

A contemporary art gallery in a Randlord's home

22 Oxford Street
Parktown
Open: The Johannesburg Heritage Foundation conducts tours that include Villa Arcadia
Check their events page for details: www.joburgheritage.org.za

The Villa Arcadia mansion in Parktown retains an aura of good taste usually reserved for the culturally well-heeled. It's hardly surprising, given that the house was commissioned in 1909 for Randlord socialites Sir Lionel and Lady Florence Phillips, colloquially known as the king and queen of Johannesburg.

From their high vantage on the ridge, the couple would have enjoyed views over the developing suburb around Saxonwold, extending as far as the purple haze of the Magaliesburg Mountains in the distance. Lady Florence was a well-known patron of the arts and was pivotal in establishing the Johanneburg Art Gallery (JAG), donating the "Founding Collection" to the gallery and rallying support for a number of cultural and patronage projects.

She also took a hands-on approach to the design of Villa Arcadia, frequently consulting with its architect, Sir Herbert Baker, over design details. Baker was revered as being meticulous, and custom ordered the red Spanish style roof tiles and other details of the estate. The couple lived in the house until 1922 when it was sold. It went on to serve as the South African Jewish Orphanage for 81 years.

In 2003, it again passed hands, this time to the Hollard Insurance company, which developed the property as its main health-conscious business campus. It has a health centre and exercise facilities for staff, while the carefully landscaped gardens host bats, Koi fish and peacocks. The campus also runs owl release and water purification projects. The villa was beautifully restored and the Italian Palazzo style marble flooring in the entrance and exquisite delft tiles of Lady Florence's bathroom remain. It now functions as a venue for meetings and events.

In keeping with the patronage of Lady Florence, Villa Arcadia showcases an impressive collection of contemporary South African artists that could rival any gallery.

Works by artists such as William Kentridge, Paul Edmunds, Conrad Botes and Jane Alexandra are shown alongside those of lesser-known artists, including a collection from Creative Block — an arts initiative for emerging artists to show and sell their works. The aim of the collection is to merge the old and the new. In acquiring works for the villa, a number of interesting collaborations were commissioned. Some of the works in the entrance, for example, were the result of a collaboration between Qubeka, a beading company, and Doreen Southwood.

THE MESSERSCHMITT 262 JET NIGHT FIGHTER

⑱

The only surviving German jet night fighter in the world

The National Museum of Military History
22 Erlswold Way
Saxonwold
Open: Daily 9am—2:30pm
Tel: 010-001-3515

Jo'burg's military museum has a complicated past. Founded in 1947 by then president Jan Smuts, it was built to be a trophy room to commemorate the country's involvement in World War Two on the side of the allies. But rife anti-British sentiment had meant that many Afrikaners were against South Africa's involvement in the war, and when the Afrikaner-led National Party won the 1948 elections, the museum was virtually mothballed.

It was only in the seventies — when South Africa was a pariah state — that the National Party began to use the museum as a propaganda tool to remind the nation that the country had once punched its weight internationally. Not surprising then that with the advent of democracy in 1994, the museum was once again left questioning its *raison d'être,* with many earmarking it as a white elephant.

This probably explains why few people know the museum is home to the only surviving two-seater German jet night fighter in the world: a Messerschmitt 262 that was used in the final defence of Berlin in 1945. With a maximum speed of 810 kph, the Messerschmitt was built to combat the RAF Mosquito. The plane on display was allocated to *Staffel 10* of the *Nachtjagdgeschwader* (the night fighter wing of the Luftwaffe), operating out of an airfield at Burg, but came too late to change the course of the war and was surrendered in Denmark in 1945. It was later transported to Britain to be deconstructed and its technology put under the microscope. German lettering on the cockpit controls has been scratched out and replaced with English words.

In 1946, South African Air Force Captain Jack Meaker was sent on a course to England. Together with colleagues from across the Commonwealth, he was taken on a tour of war spoils and told to pick whatever he wanted and it would be sent back to his country. Meaker picked the Messerschmitt. The story goes that Meaker forgot all about it, never reporting the plane to his superiors, and was surprised a few months later when, back in South Africa, he received notice that an aircraft was waiting for him at the docks in Cape Town, together with a bill for its shipping made out to Meaker himself.

The Air Force eventually agreed to pay and the plane stood in a hanger at Dunnottar Air Force Base, near Springs on the East Rand, before finally being moved to the museum in 1972, where it has been ever since.

HYDE PARK SHOPPING CENTRE ART COLLECTION

A Cecil Skotnes in a parking garage

Hyde Park Corner
Corner of Jan Smuts Avenue and William Nicol Drive
Entrance on 6th Road
Hyde Park
www.hydeparkcorner.co.za

With its quality restaurants, international brands and boutique style shops, Hyde Park is still one of Johannesburg's more upmarket shopping centres. But while its patrons continue turning up to see and be seen, the centre has modernised, and in so doing has lost some of the diamond-flecked lustre of its early hedonism.

There was a time when visiting Hyde Park meant coifing your hair, donning an "outfit" and slapping on a full face of makeup. It was not uncommon in those days to see older women, their faces stitched taught, traipsing the aisles in pearls and furs to ward against the icy chill of the summer air conditioning.

The centre was also well known for its sophisticated art collection, which formed a major part of the décor at the mall. Anyone who visited it as a child in the 1980s will remember clambering up, and sliding down, the heavy bronze sculpture by Eduardo Villa, which took pride of place in the centre court.

The Villa is long gone, but there are still hints of the mall's artistic heyday. Head downstairs to the bottom annex, and if you can push your way past the patrons squeezed into closely-packed chairs and tables, you'll find an impressive mosaicked fountain by Simon Stone.

One floor up at the movie house, past the popcorn and snacks, a 9m x 3m mosaic lines the long wall outside of the ladies and gents bathrooms. It looks dated in its neon surrounds, and given the vibrant and loud décor of the cinema chain, it's surprising the mural hasn't been pulled down. Take a close look at the signature, however, and you'll understand why the piece has survived. The clear black lettering spells out Baldinelli, the renowned Italian artist attributed with bringing mosaic art to South Africa. In the height of his career, Baldinelli's works adorned numerous important public buildings, including the old Jan Smuts Airport (now O.R. Tambo International).

But probably the most exciting (and often overlooked) find is in the car park, where a single remaining panel of what used to be an impressive frieze has survived the centre's remodelling efforts. The panel is by the late Cecil Skotnes, a pivotal 20th-century artist who is well known for having helped to shape an artistic tradition that recognised international trends while embracing a uniquely South African aesthetic. Aside from being one of South Africa's greatest artists of the time, Skotnes is also remembered for being in charge of the famous Polly Street Art Centre, which spawned young, high-calibre African artists such as Lucky Sibaya, Lucas Sithole and Sydney Kumalo.

MELVILLE WATERFALL   ⑳

A struggling green lung

Below the S-bend on Barry Hertzog Avenue
Accessible from CSIR
9th Avenue
Melville
Open: Ask guards for access

Melville is one of the favourite watering holes for the city's bohemian residents, but few of them know that there is local drinking spot that has been around for even longer than XaiXai.

Descend the steep hill of 9th Avenue and just after it crosses Rustenburg Road, but before it reaches the bridge over Barry Hertzog Avenue, take a left into the driveway of the CSIR Centre for Mining Innovation. At the bottom of their car park, behind the trees, is a path to a gushing stream, flowing down over craggy orange rocks surrounded by trees. The waterfall flows all year round, but is particularly fierce after a summer downpour.

Long before white settlers arrived in South Africa, this was the main water supply for the Tswana people, who built the Iron Age furnaces on Melville Koppies and smelted the iron they obtained from Parktown and other ridges. It would also have been the main water supply for animals living in the area, and is still home to indigenous plant species.

Later, it became an *uitvalground* (wasteland) on the wagon road to Pretoria and Rustenburg — hence how Rustenburg Road got its name. After the establishment of Melville as a suburb in 1896, it became a favourite picnic spot for the residents of Johannesburg.

The recent history of the waterfall, though, is not as romantic. The building of roads isolated the area and it was relegated to a rubble dump site.

The canalisation of the Braamfontein Spruit also changed the flow rate of the river, which impacted the ecological system.

In more recent years, its isolated nature led to the development of an informal settlement around the waterfall, bringing further pollution in the form of human waste and discarded building materials.

This settlement was moved on and for a while the site was fenced in to prevent re-settlement of the area. But when the CSIR became in danger of collapse from damp, the fences were removed to allow engineers to secure the buildings. When we visited, there was one tent in the trees, smoke rising from a campfire.

Given its historical significance, it is a pity that this spot is so little known and not preserved and treasured as a little green lung for the city, as it was by its ancient residents. Perhaps its time will come again.

HISTORIC FRENCH PRESS IN "THE ATELIER"

Manet and Degas would have printed on it

The Atelier
44 Stanley Avenue
Milpark
Tel: 011-482-2137

What do Manet, Degas and Munch have in common with a small studio and framing shop in Johannesburg? Aside from a shared passion for fine art, these masters most likely used to print editions of etches, monoprints and engravings on the same press as South African printmaker Fiona Pole.

The Press Fleury takes pride of place in the centre of Pole and partner Didier Presse's atelier, but has a history that extends back to the early days of printing in France.

"It comes from the oldest printing studio in the world and was custom built for l'Atelier Georges Leblanc in Paris," says Pole. "We've tried to trace exactly how old it is, but we're not sure. It's more than 200 years old that's certain."

Founded in 1793, the Atelier Georges Leblanc was built on the site of the Hermitage Saint Jacques, the old convent of Visitandines, which was constructed when Paris was built. Parts of the foundation and original garden were incorporated into the studio. In 1863, the Atelier was turned into a fine art etching and engraving studio. Later, under the helm of Alfred Porcaboeuf in 1894, it printed editions for the likes of Manet, Rodin, Pissario, Munch and Degas. Napoléon's *Description of Egypt* and the floral albums of Redouté were also printed at the Atelier, many of them likely on the Press Fleury.

"The amazing thing is that this press survived two world wars," says Pole. "A lot of presses were lost in the wars because just about anything metal was melted down to make arms and ammunition, but they somehow managed to save the press."

When she completed her studies at the École Estienne, Johannesburg born and raised Pole was awarded a bursary by the French City Council to work at the Atelier Georges Leblanc under the tutelage of the last owner and master printer, Pierre Lallier.

Pole lived in Paris for 13 years where she met Presse. The couple had two children. Their decision to return to South Africa coincided with the Atelier Georges Leblanc closing its doors after a long battle to save the studio from property developers.

"Pierre Lallier was such a wonderful, generous man," says Pole. "He gave me the press as a gift. And not only that, he also gave me thousands and thousands of rands worth of papers and ink so that I could start up on my own in Johannesburg."

The press was flat-packed and shipped to South Africa. It is in perfect working condition and has taken up residence at the Atelier, where it is now printing editions by South African artists.

LAM RIM TIBETAN BUDDHIST CENTRE

A haven of peace in Brixton, blessed by the Dalai Lama

1st Avenue
Brixton
Open: Thursday 7pm—8pm; Sunday 8:30am—11:30am or by appointment
Tel: Neil 082-467-5735; Philip 083-255-6089

Ask most South Africans what's the first thing that comes to mind when they hear the word Brixton, and they'll probably say "Murder and Robbery Squad". Whenever the television news asks for information in connection to a crime, it is this police station that the nation is instructed to call.

It is rather ironic then that this same neighbourhood is home to a Tibetan Buddhist temple that has been blessed by the Dalai Lama.

The Lam Rim Tibetan Buddhist Centre was established in 1993 in a derelict Dutch Reformed Church that had lost its congregation.

Brixton was one of the first suburbs to throw off apartheid segregation, and since the Dutch Reformed Church was a right-wing church that believed evidential support for apartheid could be found within the pages of the Bible (leading it to be excommunicated from the World Council of Churches), it is perhaps no surprise that with the political sea change, its parishioners fled for whiter pastures.

Today, parts of Brixton are some of the most-mixed race (and poorest) in Johannesburg.

That said, although houses may be rundown and gardens unkempt, at sunset, the streets around the temple are teeming with people walking home from work, children playing in the street, and black and white neighbours chatting over the garden fence.

"People are afraid to come here because they perceive it to be dangerous. Poor? Yes. But more dangerous? No," says Neil Hill, one of the mere five Buddhists who call this temple their spiritual home.

"I find the temple's position very helpful," he says. "In the affluent suburbs, you can forget about the city's problems. But when you drive through a rundown suburb, it helps you contemplate humility, gratitude and the opportunities that you have had in your life."

Inside, the temple is a place of immense peace. The church pews have been removed and meditation cushions are set in rows in front of a giant golden Buddha. A beautiful sand mandala — a sculpture made of sand depicting the blueprint of the celestial abode of the Buddha of compassion — made by monks who visited from Ladakh in India, sits beneath the window, while colourful silks flags drape the old church pillars.

The garden also bears a mark of the Dalai Lama: during his visit in 2004, he planted an indigenous Schotia tree, chosen because its flowers are the same saffron colour as a monk's robes and because it drips nectar, a metaphor for a blessing in Buddhist teachings.

FIETAS MUSEUM   ㉓

Among the city's secrets are many broken hearts

25 Fourteenth Street
Pageview/Fietas
Open: Monday—Thursday 10am—4pm; Saturday 10am—2pm (booking is essential)
Tel: 011-839-1566; 072-193-358

"All the born-free Indians see here is degradation and squalor, they don't know its history," says Salma Patel, 58, pointing out the many crumbling houses and empty plots piled high with rotting rubbish that line the streets of Fietas.

It wasn't always this way. Until 1976, Fourteenth Street in Fietas was "the Petticoat Lane" of Johannesburg, where Muslim merchants, who had arrived from India during the gold rush, sold luxury and everyday goods to customers of all faiths and creeds.

But like the rest of non-white South Africa, Fietas was not able to escape the segregating fist of the apartheid regime. In 1976, the Muslim traders were forcibly removed to the purpose-built Oriental Plaza. Their stores and homes were bulldozed to make way for a whites-only population.

Salma's family was one of the 67 who refused to move.

"We were the *bittereinders* (die-hards)," she says. "The fifteen blocks of this area will give you an idea of the former regime's social engineering project. They stole this for that," she says, pointing to the stark contrast between her current home — an elaborate two-storey edifice with a grand balcony, decorative columns and shimmering green tiles that was once Surtee's Silk Store — and the squat, flat-roofed white blob of a house across the road.

Salma had hoped that democracy would bring land restitution and enable Fietas to reclaim its soul. She has been bitterly disappointed by the government's failure to act. "This is a tragic, tragic place," she says.

In a bid to ease her own pain, Salma has turned the downstairs of her home into a museum, displaying mementoes of Fietas' heyday and documentary photographs of its destruction, taken by David Goldblatt and Paul Wynberg. One picture catches the eye; it is of someone standing on a ladder, painting their house white, while all around is destruction.

"That was my childhood home," Salma says with a bitter laugh. "We weren't going anywhere, and my brother was getting married. Our house was filthy, so we painted it while everything around was being destroyed."

It is a reminder that among the city's secrets are many broken hearts.

"I'm a very angry person and the way I try and assuage that is through the work I do," says Salma.

CHAMPION TREES

Heroes among giants

Gavin Reilly Green, Wits West Campus
Corner of Fawley Avenue and Lothbury Road, Auckland Park
10th Avenue, Parktown North
Thokoza Park, Soweto

"Johannesburg," we love to boast, "Is the largest urban man-made forest in the world". Come November, our jacaranda trees rival those of the capital, avocado trees provide shade and free fruit in many a back garden, and throughout the year these gentles giants provide homes to birds that make the city so much more than a concrete jungle.

But what is less known is that four of these ten million trees have been singled out by the Department of Agriculture, Forestry and Fishery as "Champion Trees" — meaning that they have both historical and cultural value, and can never be cut down.

The oldest and largest champion in Jo'burg is the eucalyptus on Wits West Campus, measuring 44-metres-tall with a canopy 38.7-metres-wide. When it was first planted over 100 years ago, the city was still a gold rush town and the site was close to the main road used by the early traders on the route between Rustenburg and Jo'burg. Today, that thoroughfare has become a lawn on Wits West Campus.

In nearby Auckland Park is a tree with political leanings. The 22 metre Lombardy poplar by the traffic lights at the entrance to Campus Square used to serve as a landmark for fugitives running from the apartheid security forces. The tree pointed out the home of Ruth Fischer, a communist party member and daughter of anti-apartheid activist and lawyer Bram Fischer, from which she operated a safe house.

Over in Parktown North is a 35-metres-high cottonwood tree, preserved as a remnant of the once semi-rural surroundings of Johannesburg that are now being built up with modern office blocks, while the newest champion is the Mandela Tree in Soweto.

Planted in Thokoza Park in 2008 by Nelson Mandela and his wife Graça Machel, the tree was intended to be a tourist attraction site, enhance socio-economic development, and add Mandela's voice to the Greening Soweto initiative. South of the mine dumps, Soweto is one part of Johannesburg that cannot be said to be part of the urban forest. But since 2006, a tree planting project with the long-term aim of planting 200,000 trees has been on the go, with the eventual aim of bringing Soweto under the canopy of the Jo'burg forest.

CHURCH OF ST. NICHOLAS OF JAPAN ㉕

A Russian missionary who wanted to take the teachings of Orthodox Christianity to Japan

154 Fulham Road
Brixton
Open: By appointment (contact Father Palmos)
Tel: 082-827-5049

Down a residential street in Brixton is a tiny white church with a shimmering gold interior, named after an unusual man.

Saint Nicholas of Japan was a Russian missionary who wanted to take the teachings of Orthodox Christianity to Japan during a time when Christianity was outlawed in the Far East nation.

On arriving in Japan he studied the local language and Japanese culture, before beginning to teach. The abiding story is that his first convert was a samurai who had been sent to kill him. The samurai was so impressed by the wise man and his sensitivity to Japanese culture that he joined forces instead, and so helped St. Nicholas convert tens of thousands of people to Orthodoxy.

Entire treatises have been written on how Orthodox Christianity differs from Roman Christianity. In essence, Orthodoxy believes God can be experienced but never fully known. The essence of God remains an enduring mystery.

Orthodox Christianity is typically associated with countries like Greece, Russia and former Yugoslavia. As such, many of the services tend to be held in the languages of these countries. In the early nineties, Father Stephen Hayes, a former Anglican minister who had converted to Orthodoxy, wanted to establish an Orthodox church in South Africa that would feel truly indigenous to the country.

"Our main thing is to be open to any ethnic group and make them feel welcome," says Father Elias Palmos, who is the current rector of the church.

Today, the congregation is small — just 50 people — but includes people from Africa, the Middle East and Eastern Europe. During a Sunday service, the Lord's Prayer is sung over and over in the languages of all people present.

Inside, the church is vibrantly painted with Byzantine iconography of angels and the Madonna and Child, all painted by South African artists.

"The style is not meant to be realistic — the images are supposed to be windows into heaven, capturing the spiritual world in two dimensions," explains Father Palmos.

There are no chairs; the congregation stands throughout the service.

"We see Sunday as a day of freedom and liberation. To kneel is to be in servitude, a form of penance. The intention is for people to feel free."

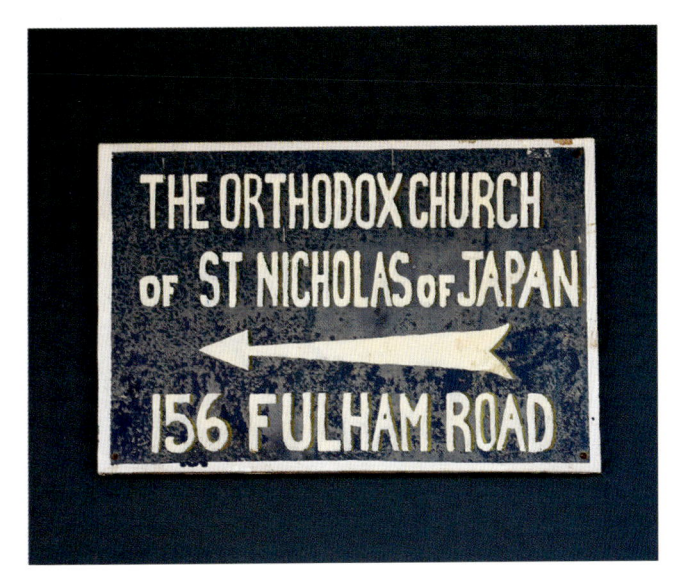

LINDFIELD VICTORIAN HOUSE MUSEUM

Victoria's Secret and other curiosities

72 Richmond Avenue
Auckland Park
Open: By appointment only
Tel: 011-726-2932
www.lindfield.wix.com/museum

The Lindfield Victorian House Museum, a private home in Auckland Park, is an Aladdin's cave packed with wonderful, quirky, ostentatious and just plain weird Victoriana. The most fascinating of the lot lies in the heart of the home in a narrow, rectangular room aptly named the "cabinet of curiosities".

It's here, tucked into a glass display case, that you'll find what might well be the very first example of "Victoria's Secret" — a yellowing piece of lace that once graced the nether regions of Queen Victoria herself.

"The old lady who gave it to my mother told us that her great grandmother worked in the house of the royal family as a wet nurse. She was given the lace by her friend who was one of the queen's dressers," says Katharine Love, owner of the living museum.

One of the perks of being a dresser was that they inherited the off-cast clothing of the royal family. It's not clear what the savvy servants did with the finery they were given, but the bloomers were cut into squares, neatly hemmed and sold as souvenirs.

"My mother started collecting antiques as a child and started this museum 40 years ago," says Love, who has lived in the house since she was thirteen. She inherited her mother's passion for all things Victoriana and continued the legacy of obsessive collecting after her mother's death in 1996.

The house, actually an Edwardian style home built in 1910, has been accurately converted to represent a British upper middle-class home of the Victorian era, replete with myriad exotic collectibles that appealed to the aristocracy of the time. "They loved pretty things and loved collecting and they loved the exotic," says Love. "Rich families would initially pay explorers to bring back items from far off lands."

A tour at Lindfield is unusual. Although Love follows a standard route through her home, it is so jam-packed with fascinating objects that guests set the pace according to their interests. Find yourself captivated by a first edition of *Mrs Beeton's Book of Household Management*? Love will let you know that the author to this housewives' tome was a mere 21-years-old when she started writing it. Ghoulishly fascinated by a Tibetan Damaru drum? She'll let you know that it's made from the skulls and skin of venerated monks.

"I just love the whole thing. People all ask me such different questions," she says. "They often ask questions I just hadn't thought about before."

THE PARANOID TREE

A metaphor for Johannesburg

Melville Koppies Central
Judith Road
Open: Access by appointment only; Group walks every Sunday
Email: fomk@mk.org.za

High up in Melville Koppies Central is a metaphor for Johannesburg: the *Parinari Capensis*, aka the paranoid tree.

In a city where so many of its residents are hidden behind high walls, electric fences and car windows, this tree acts like a real Joburger; its roots, trunk and branches grow entirely inside the orange quartzite rocks, with only its leaf canopy visible at toe height. While it is crime that worries the humans of Johannesburg, it is anxiety over fire, frost, grazing, drought and flood that sent the tree into hiding.

Melville Koppies Central is also something of a secret. The Koppies spans open grasslands and damp acacia woodlands, but concerns over opportunistic crime have led to this designated nature reserve and Iron Age heritage site being fenced and locked, with visits only possible escorted by a guide and a guard. Friends of the Melville Koppies host group walks every Sunday.

"This is our enchanted forest," confides volunteer caretaker and guide Wendy Carstens, pointing at a tree thick with lichen. "This is where the fairies come to party. They live in the Water Tower in Northcliff and the Hadedas bring them here at night."

Thanks to Carstens' vision, the reserve has been thoroughly weeded of alien plants and transformed into an indigenous wilderness in the heart of the city, giving visitors a glimpse of Jo'burg before the gold rush.

Surrounding the paranoid tree are over fifty types of grass, wild dagga (its sweet orange blooms popular with sunbirds), fever tree bushes, African wormwood, an abundance of *Protea Kaffra*, with its electric pink flowers, and Buffalo thorn trees, also known as the *Llalapansi*, or "rest well", because its branches are placed inside Sotho and Tswana graves to help the soul pass to the other side.

Another plant with a story is the Everlasting Bush. Its scent of manly aftershave meant it was traditionally mixed with goat fat and worn by young Zulu men to attract the ladies.

On the northern face of the Koppies are ruins of stone kraals, an Iron Age furnace and a display of ancient iron farming tools, remnants of a time when the area was home to Bantu sheep and cattle farmers, who mined the rocks for iron after migrating to the Highveld in 1550AD in search of better pastures.

GAUTENG'S ARTESIAN SPRING

A refreshing find

Albert's Farm Conservancy
Corner of 8th and 6th Roads
Albert's Kroon

Johannesburg is a historically water poor region. It also shares the distinction with Birmingham in England of being one of only two cities in the world that are not built around a harbour or river. With an ever-increasing population and growing industry, the city and surrounds rely heavily on the engineering feat of the Lesotho Highlands Water Project to source water from our neighbouring country to prevent the city from running dry.

Major rivers that run through the CBD and informal settlements are heavily polluted. So to find a natural source of pure, clean spring water on the outskirts of the city is, if nothing else, refreshing.

Aside from being a beautiful park with rolling natural grasslands, rocky outcrops and a small dam for fishing, Albert's Farm is home to Gauteng's only artesian spring.

Situated towards the north-western edge of the park is a wooden bridge that leads into a small oasis of red hot pokers (*Kniphofia Moench*), Louisiana water irises (*Iris Louisiana*) and various reeds. Follow the sounds of trickling water to find the source of the spring, which runs year round with fantastic tasting, earth-sprung clean water.

A spring is usually formed when underground water moving through permeable layers hits an impermeable layer of rock and is forced to the surface. In the case of the Albert's Farm artesian spring, south-facing shale meets a downward-sloping quartz rock from the north, which forms an impenetrable basin in which the water collects and is forced to the surface.

The 90ha park is Johannesburg's second largest green lung (surpassed only by Delta Park) and is deliberately managed to retain a natural state, which affords the unusual opportunity to view Jo'burg's distinctive skyline through long veld grass. It is also ecologically significant and a welcome retreat for nature lovers who can look out for about 29 grass species, 60 indigenous shrubs, 35 indigenous tree species and about 140 bird species.

The parkland was sold to the city by the Albert family in 1946 for £18,500 on the condition that it be used for the enjoyment of the public. One hundred and seventy one years later, the city has kept its promise and the park bustles on weekends with a weekly Park Run, picnickers and the rhythmic drumming and singing of worshippers who come to the dam for prayer and baptism.

TREVOR HUDDLESTON'S CENOTAPH

㉙

A community saint sleeps among multiracial angels

Church of Christ the King
49 Ray Street
Sophiatown
Tel: 011-477-8410

At the highest point in Sophiatown, within the Church of Christ the King, a mosaic cenotaph depicting Archbishop Trevor Huddleston in his black robes is inscribed with the words: *What is the meaning of life?* It is a wonderful spot to contemplate the past and the present; Sophiatown was the place that the apartheid government first flexed its muscle, forcibly removing the black, Indian, Chinese and coloured residents in the years between 1955 and 1962, sending them to live in newly created, racially designated suburbs. In their wake, their homes were destroyed and a whites-only suburb named *Triomf* (Triumph) was built in its place.

In the years leading up to the forced removals, then Reverend Trevor Huddleston, a white Anglican minister from England, was regarded as the defender of the people of Sophiatown.

From 1943 to 1956, Sophiatown was a hotbed of political activism, where a young Nelson Mandela, Walter Sisulu and Oliver Tambo would frequently meet in the home of Dr. Xuma, then president of the ANC. From his church — where the altar was framed by a mural of black and white angels sitting together at the feet of Jesus — Huddleston fought to stop the removals, earning himself the nickname *Makhalipile* (the dauntless one). His outspoken protest led church authorities to fear for his safety; in 1956, he was recalled to England, where he went on to lead the anti-apartheid movement in the UK.

After the area was demolished, Huddleston's church was deconsecrated and turned into a recreation hall for the new whites-only community. Today, the beautiful multiracial mural seems to be lost forever, defaced by the members of the Triomf boxing club and hidden beneath a coat of white paint. But some of the old faces are back; behind the altar is a mosaic of a black Jesus surrounded by the many characters of 1950s Sophiatown, jubilant and hugging, depicting the long journey to reconciliation. Every Sunday, a bus brings in the former community from Meadowlands to worship in their old church. And then there is Huddleston who returned for the last time in June 1998, after his death, to become the eternal guardian of Sophiatown.

SOPHIATOWN'S HERITAGE TREE ㉚

The tree with the soul of Sophiatown

St. Joseph's Diocesan Centre
Corner of Good and Herman Streets
Christ the King Church
49 Ray Street
Sophiatown
The Mix
71 to 73 Toby Street
Tel: 011-673-1271
www.sophiatownthemix.com

"Aaaaai, but that tree was huge," says Sophiatown resident Ma Elizabeth, branching her arms wildly to demonstrate its expanse. "It covered up to the middle of the street, and it dirtied up the place. You would sweep every hour, and it would be so full of leaves again, it would look like no one was living here."

The tree, an enormous 100-year-old English oak on her neighbour's property on Bertha Street, was a well-known landmark of old Sophiatown. With a girth of 4.48 metres and a crown width of more than 30 metres, the tree became a gathering point for political meetings in the tumultuous 1950s. At that time, Sophiatown was a mixed-race neighbourhood made famous as a hub of resistance politics, gangsters, jazz and drinking. It was home to some of South Africa's greatest writers, musicians, politicians and artists.

"There was so much activity, people driving around in big American cars, dressed in fancy clothes. One of my uncles played the trumpet with [famous pennywhistle musician] Spokes Mashiyani. Every Sunday they would arrive at our house, and people would come to watch them perform. These are very good memories I still have."

Ma Elizabeth was seven when the apartheid government began the forced removal of Sophiatown's residents to make way for the all-whites enclave of Triomph.

The trauma shattered the community, and the oak took on an ominous role as a suicide tree after two people hung themselves from its branches rather than face removal.

After democracy, some of the original residents, including Ma Elizabeth, trickled back to the suburb, and in 2004 the oak became the first tree in Johannesburg to be protected under law after the Bertha Street property owner threatened to cut it down.

In 2007 the tree died amid speculation that the property owner may have poisoned it. Now the remnants of that tree can be found around Sophiatown. Two prominent chunks live beside the parking lot at the St. Joseph's Diocesan Centre (formerly St. Joseph's Home for Coloured Children).

The main stump, which lived at Sophiatown, The Mix (formerly the Sophiatown Heritage Centre) for many years, now stands in the studio of artist Tendai Sithole, who was commissioned in 2015 to sculpt three figureheads: Nelson Mandela, Alfred Xuma and Trevor Huddleston.

The Department of Water Affairs and Forestry managed to grow a singular seedling cultivated from the original tree. Its planting was originally intended for 2009, but the department abandoned the plans with the change of minister, according to Tricia Sibbons of Sophiatown, The Mix. The sapling was eventually planted in late 2017 and now stands in the Christ the King churchyard, waiting, much like Sophiatown, to grow to a new kind of glory.

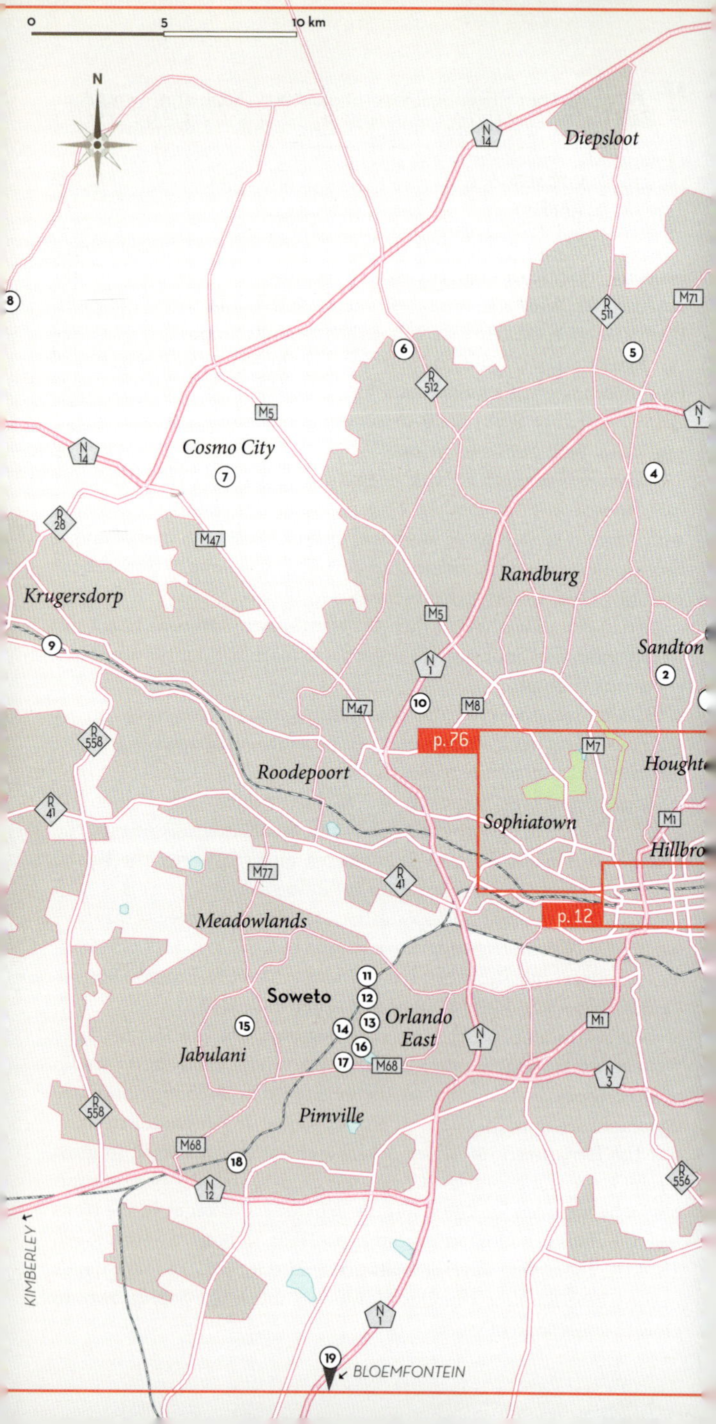

0
5
10 km
N
Diepsloot
N 14
8
R 511
M71
6
5
R 512
M5
N 1
N 14
Cosmo City
7
4
R 28
M47
Randburg
Krugersdorp
M5
9
Sandton
N 1
2
M47
10
M8
R 558
p. 76
M7
Houghton
Roodepoort
R 41
M1
Sophiatown
Hillbrow
M77
R 41
p. 12
Meadowlands
11
Soweto
12
M1
Orlando East
15
14
13
N 1
16
Jabulani
17
M68
N 3
R 558
Pimville
M68
18
N 12
R 556
KIMBERLEY
N 1
19
BLOEMFONTEIN

Greater Joburg: Soweto, North and West

①	EDOARDO'S VILLA	140
②	GARDEN OF ST. CHRISTOPHER	142
③	EDOARDO VILLA'S "CONFRONTATION" SCULPTURE	144
④	MANDELA'S MISSING PISTOL	146
⑤	IRON AGE FURNACES BURIED IN A PARK	148
⑥	JFK MEMORIAL	150
⑦	ROBERT "SPILLER" VAN TONDER GRAVE	152
⑧	MOGALE'S GATE BIODIVERSITY CENTRE	154
⑨	NAMELESS GRAVES OF THE BURGERSHOOP CEMETERY	156
⑩	MTN ART COLLECTION	158
⑪	LILIAN NGOYI MEMORIAL	160
⑫	THE CRADLE OF SOWETO	162
⑬	ORLANDO PIRATES PAINTING	164
⑭	BIRD WATCHING IN SOWETO	166
⑮	CREDO MUTWA VILLAGE	168
⑯	ANTI-XENOPHOBIA SCULPTURES	170
⑰	ENOCH SONTONGA HILL	172
⑱	SS MENDI MEMORIAL	174
⑲	THE SHARPEVILLE HUMAN RIGHTS PRECINCT	176

EDOARDO'S VILLA

The suburban home of a legendary sculptor

75 4th Road
Kew
Open: By appointment only
Email: enquiries@warrensiebrits.co.za

When Edoardo Villa passed away at the age of 95 in 2011, the trust set up in his name was determined to preserve his home for prosperity. As one of South Africa's most prolific and famous artists of the 20th century, they felt it important to save the home, studio and gardens where Villa had created his large-scale metal sculptures.

The trust approached art dealer, collector and consultant Warren Siebrits and his wife Lunetta Bartz with the aim of selling the house to someone who would respect the legacy of the late artist. Aside from owning a number of Villa's pieces, Siebrits knew the artist well, having forged a long-term friendship, sparked through a series of coincidences.

"When I was first starting out in the art world at Sotheby's, I bought Villa's 1970 Audi coupe in about 1992. I bought it via a friend and for some reason we never got around to transferring ownership.

"I was young, living in Yeoville and raced around Jo'burg in that car, running up [speeding] fines. One day I got this slightly concerned, but furious phone call from Edoardo, who had received a number of fines and a summons to court. I went to court and ended up paying about R1000, which was a fortune in those days.

"It was a real wake-up call for me, but it's also how I got to meet Edoardo. Years later, in 1999, when I met him again [at an art function], he asked me, 'Do you still have the car? You know, I really wanted to kill you.'"

Villa originally bought the Kew property in 1959 and lived and worked from a cold, damp cottage. Later, in 1968, when the damp became a real concern and he began to make money through his art, he approached his architect friend Ian McLennan to come up with something interesting. His budget was a meagre R13,121.

The result was a relatively small home with a large feel, thanks to its modernist open-plan design and large plate glass windows. The rough interior surfaces create textured backdrops to art works, enhanced by the light that filters through skylights, while the exterior cladding has weathered over the years and developed a beautiful patina from the rain.

Aside from being a tribute to the artist, the house is a comfortable weekend home for its owners and a venue for art functions. Siebrits is happy to show people around by appointment and it makes for an interesting visit for anyone interested in architecture or art. Aside from getting a glimpse into the artist's world, Siebrits is a storybook of information about Villa and South African art in general.

GARDEN OF ST. CHRISTOPHER

A garden of Italianate delights

Hyde Park
Address by request
Open to the public for one day a year, usually in October, for a «spring opening». Ticket numbers are limited to around 1,500.
The rest of year, visits during the week are by appointment only. No visiting at weekends.

In the seven-acre grounds of a Jo'burg Tuscan manor house, is an unexpected slice of Renaissance Italy.

Each part of the garden has a distinct personality: a more formal garden and rolling green lawn closer to the mansion house, water fountains, an orchard and a parterre (a knee-high hedged maze) halfway down, before going on to become wilder in the far corners with a bee and butterfly garden, a camellia walk (with hundreds of camellias rescued from a nursery that was closing down), and a waterfall made from hunks of Tiger's Eye rock.

The rock is not the only semi-precious stone in the garden. The homeowner's passion for mining, as well as flowers, is reflected by the enormous chunks of rose quartz, cactus quartz, butter jade and hematite woven among the plants, creating a "gem walkway". Also unique to the garden is the stumpery — an idea borrowed from Victorian formal gardens, which was resurrected by Prince Charles in his garden at Highgrove. Here, the stumps of dead trees are flipped and ferns are planted into their roots, creating living sculptural creations.

"It is a nice way to remember the trees that we have to take down," says Allison Nicholson, the horticulturalist and garden designer who works full-time alongside eight permanent gardeners and the foreman, Walter Maphalala, who has been with the garden since its inception and knows the mood of every plant in this garden, according to Nicholson.

It is also a dog-friendly garden and Nicholson's sidekick, a rusty Labrador, clearly regards the oval mirror pond with its Heron sculpture as its private swimming pool.

The Garden of St. Christopher, so named because he was the patron saint of gardening as well as travel, is the passion project of the homeowner (who prefers to go unnamed) and is open to the public for only one day of the year.

Throughout the rest of the year, it welcomes gardening enthusiasts on tours from Australia, Britain and the US. It also offers short courses in rose pruning, container planting, skills development for domestic gardeners, and creating gardens in smaller spaces.

All income raised from the garden is donated to Johannesburg Child Welfare and Guide Dogs for the Blind.

EDOARDO VILLA'S "CONFRONTATION" SCULPTURE

③

Art that confronts the system

Behind Rand Merchant Bank building
Rivonia Road
Sandton

Surrounded by water, palm trees and towering blocks of finance is South Africa's Guernica: Edoardo Villa's response to the 1976 Soweto uprising.

Villa had been a prisoner of war. He had been captured in Sidi Barrani in Egypt and sent to Zonderwater POW camp in South Africa, where he had four years to reflect on how efficient the Fascist propaganda machine had been.

He had expected the POW camp to be a grim experience, but it turned out to be the beginning of new insights and opportunities.

The head of the camp, Captain Henry Sonneband, believed the prisoners should be put to purposeful work, and since Villa was a classically trained artist, he was encouraged to do arts and crafts and even occasionally allowed to visit the art galleries of Jo'burg and Pretoria.

After the war, all POWs were ordered back to their native lands. But Villa did not want to return to war-torn Italy. Instead, he went underground in South Africa and continued to make art under the radar.

His early sculpture work emulated Africa, as if the young artist was trying to identify himself in his new landscape. But as the years went on and the political situation in South Africa intensified, so did the politics in his work. "This sculpture, titled "Confrontation", expressed the deep unease in the country post the Soweto uprising. Before that time, art and politics were not as enmeshed as they became in the 1980s," explains Karel Nel, artist and associate professor of visual art at the University of Witwatersrand, who co-authored a book on Villa's prolific career.

"He was a free thinker and wanted others to be the same," says Nel, adding that Villa's own history had given him a keen sense of *"La lotta per la vita"* (the struggle for life).

Villa made "Confrontation" without the support of a sponsor or backer.

"He stretched his own resources to the limit to make it happen, because of a conviction that he ought to, somehow, reflect the impending crisis he senses from the experience," says Nel.

Today, though, its significance goes unnoticed by many of the local office workers.

"To me, it doesn't say anything about the 1970s. It's just a thing that's there. Maybe someone should put a sign up to explain," suggests Busi Mthembu, who works close by. "In Soweto where they died, the pavements are painted red, which is supposed to be the blood, but until someone explains that, it's like, so what."

MANDELA'S MISSING PISTOL

A lost piece of the liberation struggle

Liliesleaf
7 George Avenue
Rivonia
Open: Monday—Friday 8:30am—5pm; weekends and public holidays 9am—4pm
Tel: 011-803-7882/3/4

In 1961, Nelson Mandela — head of the ANC's newly formed armed wing, Umkhonto we Sizwe — went into hiding. The South African Communist Party had bought Liliesleaf, a smallholding in Rivonia, which was then a rural area on the far edge of the city. In October that year, the "Black Pimpernel", aka Mandela, moved in, posing as houseboy and caretaker David Motsamayi.

Two months later, a white family — Arthur and Hazel Goldreich and their two children — joined him to give the illusion that this was just a normal family home and not the headquarters of the resistance movement.

In January 1962, Mandela secretly left South Africa to attend the Pan-African Freedom movement for East, Central and Southern Africa Conference in Addis Ababa, as well as to undergo military training.

When he returned to Liliesleaf, he brought with him an automatic pistol and 200 rounds of ammunition, a gift from the Ethiopian Colonel Tadesse, who had lectured him on military science. The pistol was thought to be a Bulgarian Makarov. Mandela buried it for safekeeping. "We dug a pit, deep enough that a plough wouldn't cover it, then wrapped the stuff in tin alloy and plastic, and put a layer of ground over it and a tin plate so the rain couldn't get in, and covered it with soil," Mandela recalled 40 years later.

In 1962, in Howick, on his way back from visiting Chief Albert Luthuli, then leader of the ANC, Mandela was arrested. He was sentenced to five years' imprisonment. Things went from bad to worse on 11 July 1963, when the police raided Liliesleaf, intercepting a meeting of the ANC top brass. During the raid, police uncovered incriminating documents, which were later used in the Rivonia Trial to sentence the leaders of the struggle to life imprisonment.

The pistol, however, remains missing to this day.

"We've had all sorts of people looking for it, with metal detectors, and specialists from overseas," says Tracey Rapelego, a tour guide at Liliesleaf, which has since been turned into a museum to the struggle movement. "I think we've given up now."

But while the real secret may be lost underground, Rapelego thinks that Liliesleaf itself is a forgotten treasure to many South Africans.

"We get so few local visitors," she says. "When I tell people I work at Liliesleaf, they ask, 'Do you sell flowers there?'"

IRON AGE FURNACES BURIED IN A PARK

⑤

*One of the finest Iron Age smelting
and forging sites dating back to 1600AD*

Lonehill Nature Reserve
7 Cresent Drive
Lonehill
Open: Saturdays, Sundays and public holidays 8am—6pm

Until about 25 years ago, the northern suburb of Lonehill retained echoes of Johannesburg's natural past, comprising largely small holdings surrounded by veldt. But suburban sprawl has filled the area with townhouse developments and gated communities. The only remaining evidence of its natural abundance lies in a prominent koppie surrounded by a small reserve and parkland.

Based on an Anglo Boer War fable stating that if the Boers dislodged a precariously positioned boulder at the peak of the koppie, the Brits would lose the war and leave, a modern legend claims that if the rock is ever toppled, all the whites will leave the country.

The rock, however, remains firmly in place, having witnessed generations of human folly dating right back to the Iron Age — although we will have to take an archeologist's word for it. In the 1960s, the former head of archeology at Wits University, Professor Revil Mason, unearthed one of the finest and most complete Iron Age smelting and forging sites dating back to 1600AD. He also found evidence of rocks used for grinding, pottery manufacture and stone kraals. At the time, Mason was conducting research into ancient settlements in what is now urban and suburban Johannesburg. He found evidence of settlements in Melville and Northcliff in the west, Bruma in the east, Lonehill in the North and Klipriviersberg in the South.

Based on the patterns found on pottery fragments, the settlers were likely Sotho or Tswana speakers who chose the koppies due to the abundance of ferricrete (high in iron salts) in the nearby Jukskei Spruit, and because the air currents moving up the koppie were ideal for smelting.

There was little chance of human disruption in Lonehill at the time, but Mason, perhaps with an eye to the future, wisely decided to hide the furnaces. There was no funding available to adequately protect them and he no doubt decided this was their only chance of long-term survival.

Since Lonehill's development, the koppies have been fenced in and are surrounded by a 20 hectare plot, which is locked during the week but opened during weekends and public holidays, allowing walkers and picnickers to enjoy the small piece of natural space available to them. But when stamping around the well laid out pathways or picnicking, it's unlikely that people know they are quite possibly traipsing over a piece of ancestral gold.

JFK MEMORIAL

⑥

The only memorial to an American president in South Africa

Witkoppen Primary School
Plot 110, William Nicol Drive
Fourways
Open: By appointment
Tel: 011-705-3011

Witkoppen Primary school, just down the road from the busy Fourways Mall, houses the only memorial to an American president in South Africa.

The school started life in 1942 as a missionary school. But in 1953, as a protest against the introduction of Bantu Education by the apartheid state, the Anglican bishop ordered it closed.

Pupils of the school were mostly children of the local farm workers. Parents and the farm manager were outraged; to their minds, no school was worse than Bantu education, explains current headmaster Mr. Makama. They approached H.F. Verwoerd, then in charge of education, asking for the school to be reopened.

It was, but it had few resources. For every white child who attended, the government paid R100. For every black child it paid R25.

Over the coming decades, the school was taken under the wing of the Engelharts, who were Anglo-American representatives in South Africa and friends of John F. Kennedy. With the help of JFK, they ensured the school had adequate funding for teaching resources, water and electricity, stipends for the teachers, and food, clothes and transport for the children — some of whom came from as far away as Muldersdrift.

One notable pupil to come out of the school was Dr. C.N. Phatudi, who later translated Shakespeare into Sepedi and became part of the traditional leadership in Leboa.

After JFK died and the Engelharts left the country, Mary Slack, one of the Oppenheimer daughters, made sure that the school continued to have the funding it needed.

Today the school falls under the remit of the Gauteng Education department, though there are still echoes of a time gone by.

The vegetable garden once used to teach farm skills to farm labourers' children is now used for teaching children with special needs, including Down's syndrome, severe and mild mental disability and hearing impairment.

On the office wall is a framed photograph of Jackie Kennedy, signed "To the children of Witkoppen, with deepest good wishes", while above the out-of-tune piano in the school chapel (which doubles as a classroom) is a marble sign that reads, "In Memory of John Fitzgerald Kennedy, President of the United States".

The marble memorial was installed after JFK's assassination.

ROBERT "SPILLER" VAN TONDER GRAVE

⑦

The most unlikely grave in Cosmo City

In front of Oasis centre
814 Georgia Crescent
Cosmo City

Ons hulde aan: Entrepeneur
Skrywer
Digter
Vader
Oupa
Eggenoot
Geliefde volks-
Leier

6 Oktober 1923-
4 Augustus 1999

Oom Robert

ROBERT SPILLER VAN TONDER

Agter kleinseun van prof. Dirk Postma, stigter van die Gereformeerde kerk in Suid Afrika.

Seun en kleinseun van Boere-vryheidsvegters wat geveg het in die Engelse Oorlog 1899-1902.

Sy verbete stryd vir die handhawing van Afrikaans besorg hom die ere-titel 'TAALBUL VAN TONDER'

Stigterslid van die HNP

Sy filosofie is opgesluit in volkskap en die verskyning van sy boek "BOERESTAAT" (1977) bevestig sy status as die VADER VAN DIE BOERESTAAT filosofie nl. "Die herstel van die eertydse Boere Republieke van Transvaal Vrystaat en Vryheid in 'n moderne Boerestaat".

Stigter en leier van die Boerestaat party

Stigter van die dorp Randburg (1959)

Gewaardeerde eggenoot van Sussie Steyn (1951-1973) en Louisa Richter (1981-1999).

Geliefde vader van Hans, Thomas, Elna, Alet, Robert, Addriaan en Dirk.

Oupa van 17 kleinkinders.

VRYHEID AAN ALLE VOLKE   OOK AAN DIE BOEREVOLK!
DIE STRYD DUUR VOORT..............

In the far north of Johannesburg, in the fields of an old farm, is a new city: Cosmo City (Cosmo being short for cosmopolitan). In 2004, the foundation stones were laid for what was to be Jo'burg's first purpose-built integrated suburb. There would be bigger properties for the middle classes (on streets named after American states: Alabama, Tennessee, Georgia), smaller builds for first-time home owners (on South Korea, Bangladesh and Cambodia Crescents) and clusters of squat, square RDP houses — free government housing for those who previously squatted in shacks (built on streets named Angola, Zimbabwe and Congo).

It was to be a post-apartheid model suburb to accommodate all races. What made it even more of a new South Africa tale, was the land it was to be built on — land that had belonged to the ABSA bank and an old farm of Boer nationalist Robert "Spiller" van Tonder.

Van Tonder was descended from Boer War commandoes who felt betrayed by the outcome of the Anglo-Boer War — they did not want a unified South Africa and felt the Boers were better off on their own. In 1977, van Tonder published his book *Boerestaat*, in which he laid out his philosophy for a new Boer republic, earning him the nickname *Taalbul* (one who fights for their language). For years van Tonder has used his isolated farm — distinguished by a vast Vierkleur flag at its entrance — as the headquarters from which to wage a battle for the restoration of the old Boer Republics.

Unsurprisingly, van Tonder did not want to sell. To obtain the land, the City was required to use existing legislation to expropriate the land for the public benefit. This was a very drawn-out process with a lot of public participation and thousands of objectors. The City eventually won, but van Tonder remained. When he died in 1999, he was buried on his farm, now a short walk from the Cosmo City Kentucky Fried Chicken. On his grey marble tombstone, next to his thatched farm chapel (now a computer centre teaching IT skills to the local youth) is the inscription: *Vryheid Aan Alle Volke. Ook Aan die Boerevolke. Die Stryd Duur Voort* — Freedom for All People. Also for the Boers. The Struggle Continues. It's doubtful he is resting in peace.

MOGALE'S GATE BIODIVERSITY CENTRE

The second most biodiverse biome in South Africa

The Cradle of Humankind
Open: By appointment only
Tel: 014-576-2091/2375

Most people visit the Cradle of Humankind for what lies beneath the ground: a fossil-rich labyrinth of caves and sinkholes that has astounded archaeologists with its treasures. It was here that the first complete Australopithecus skull was discovered (affectionately called Mrs. Ples), while more recently, the discovery of "Little Foot", a 3.3-million-year-old almost complete ape-man skeleton, made international headlines.

What is less acknowledged, however, is that the 180 square miles of Highveld that sit above the 15 paleontological sites are themselves somewhat special.

South Africa has 10 per cent of all the plant species in the world, spread across nine different biomes (plant and animal habitats), and two of these biomes intersect in the Cradle: the grasslands of the high inland plateau and the sub-Saharan savannah of the low inland plateau.

We often hear how South Africa's Fynbos biome has the highest biodiversity in the world, but the grasslands come in at a close second, making the Cradle an area of immense biodiversity.

Grasslands are typically found in areas that experience regular frost and fire (without these, the veld would transform into savannah), and the Cradle has had a long love affair with fire. It is believed that it was here that humans first learnt to harvest fire from the frequent lightning strikes.

That said, grasslands are the most threatened of all of South Africa's biomes as most of the country's farming and cities are developed on this productive land.

Living within this rich area, just 50 minutes drive from the inner city, are 19 game species, including the threatened and protected black wildebeest, oribi, and giant bullfrog; it is home to predators such as the caracal, leopard, black-backed jackal and brown hyena; and over 270 bird species including the martial eagle, secretary bird and Cape vulture.

Just next door to the well-trodden driveway to the Maropeng Visitor Centre is the lesser-known Mogale's Gate Biodiversity Centre, which is on the ecotone between the two biomes, and which is not only a refuge for this immense diversity of plant and animal species, but also a place where Joburgers can go, by appointment, to hike and take a class in the bush school.

As the city continues to mushroom and spawn new townhouse complexes further and further afield, it's crucial that we acquire a better understanding of the incredible treasure trove right on our doorstep.

NAMELESS GRAVES OF THE BURGERSHOOP CEMETERY

Relics of the Anglo-Boer Wars

Wagen Street
Krugersdorp
Open: 8am—5pm every day

On the western flank of Krugersdorp's Burgershoop (meaning 'citzen's hope') Cemetery, are rows of nameless graves, each headstone inscribed only with the words *"KonsentrasieKamp, 1899-1902 Rus in vrede"*. It is here that some of the 28,000 women and children who died in the British concentration camps of the Second Anglo-Boer War, now renamed the South African War, are buried.

It was a guerrilla war. "The women were supplying the fighting men with food and arms, so they became a legitimate target of war. The British put them into camps to stop the supply chain," explains amateur historian Rod Kruger, who passionately documents the stories of this part of Johannesburg.

Prior to this, Boer women and children had lived on isolated farms, and when put together in the world's first concentration camps, many of them died from diseases to which they lacked immunity, including measles and whooping cough.

To fight against the guerrillas the British also devised a complex network of blockhouses and barbed wire fences in order to partition and watch over conquered territory.

Nowadays, the former concentration camp is a children's play park and dam, while Fort Harlech, the stone blockhouse that overlooked the camp (now on Sarel Oosthuizen Street), is an electrical substation, itself surrounded with barbed wire.

Three kilometres away, behind an electric fence, and accessible only by appointment (tel: 083-227-3260), is another Boer relic — the Paardekraal Monument. After gold was discovered, the British annexed the Transvaal without any initial resistance from the Boers. Three years later, at the suggestion of Paul Kruger, the Boers gathered in Krugersdrop, each carrying a rock from their farms. They piled the rocks and made a vow to defeat the British. Ten years after the First Anglo-Boer War, they built the Paardekraal Monument over the rocks to mark their victory. But it did not last. The Boers lost the Second Anglo-Boer War and during the campaign the Brits took the rocks from under the monument and threw them off a bridge into the Vaal River. There they remained until infamous right-wing politician Clive Derby-Lewis tracked them down shortly before he was jailed for his assassination of the Communist Party leader Chris Hani. "At first he couldn't find the rocks, but then he realised the bridge had moved. He went to the site of the original bridge and found a bunch of rocks, all so distinctly different rocks, they could only be the vow rocks," says the Paardekraal committee's Assistant Laer Kommandant, Sid Mann. Derby-Lewis kept them first in his garage, before they were returned to the monument, where they now lie.

MTN ART COLLECTION

The transition-era art collection

MTN Innovation Centre
216, 14th Avenue
Fairland
Open: Monday—Friday by appointment only
Tel: 083-222-5325

The cellular telephone revolution coincided with South Africa's transition to democracy, making MTN one of the country's few companies without a complicated past. In 1997, in a bid to bring emerging black artists into the mainstream economy and show that it was a socially conscious company that was sensitive to the country's socio-political history, MTN began collecting art.

During the first few years, MTN prolifically collected nearly 1,000 artworks by South African and African artists around the theme "The Road Ahead". The company employed a team of specialists and curators to exhibit the collection to staff and the public in order to spark dialogue and debate and to create several art educational resources for teachers and learners.

Unfortunately, the heyday period of art collecting was stifled by the global financial crisis and now, 20 years after the collection's inception, it has receded from regular public view in Johannesburg.

Notable works include Tony Nkotsi's "Portrait of a Man" (a linocut of Steve Biko holding the key to South Africa) and cutting-edge contemporary pieces by artists from the African diaspora commenting on a variety of subjects from domestic violence (Trevor Makhoba's "It's Dad, Mum"), decolonisation (Yinka Shonibare's "Diary of a Victorian Dandy") and resistance to political oppression (Kwesi Owusu-Ankomah's "Soft Gentle Depths"), along with a 140-piece collection of resistance posters.

Sole manager of the art collection Niel Nortje arranges four internal exhibitions a year mostly themed around international and South African public holidays: Human Rights Day, Freedom Day, Youth Day, Woman's Day, Heritage Day, 16 Days of Activism against gender based violence and child abuse, and World Aids Day. However, he has found that the office walls are not always the best place for such a dynamic collection.

"If something disturbs or moves you at an art gallery, you can choose to turn away, leave the gallery and think about it later. But if you get upset about an artwork in your work space, you can't always walk away and feel forced to engage," says Nortje, adding that in MTN's previous Sandton office, they used to hang the most challenging works in "controversy corridor", a spur hallway that people could choose either to engage with or avoid. In their current campus, each internal exhibition is accompanied by guided tours and walkabouts to explain controversial artworks and to improve visual literacy among staff.

LILIAN NGOYI MEMORIAL

A stitch in time

9870b Nkungu Street
Mzimhlope
Soweto

On a small wall outside a small house in Mzimhlope, Soweto, is a unique memorial to a unique woman.

Lilian Ngoyi joined the ANC in 1950 during the Defiance Campaign. She soon became elected as the President of the ANC Women's League. In the early fifties, she slipped out of the country and went to Europe where she visited a Nazi concentration camp. From her later writings, it is clear that visit strengthened her resolve to stand up to violence and oppression.

On 9 August 1956, Ngoyi was one of four women who led the women's march on the Union Buildings in Pretoria to protest the extension of the apartheid pass laws to African woman.

Her political commitment made her a target of the apartheid government. She was first arrested in December 1956 and charged with treason, along with 156 other political leaders, including Nelson Mandela. Much of the next 30 years of her life was spent in detention, often in solitary confinement for months at a time. She was banned from attending any social gatherings or political meetings and confined to her home under the Suppression of Communism Act.

Not that Ngoyi always obeyed the banning orders. She broke her very first banning order in the early sixties by holding a party in her house (attended by the late Walter Sisulu and Alfred Nzo), for which she spent a weekend in jail.

Later, she would disguise herself as an old lady to go and visit friends, and she attended her brother's funeral disguised as an Indian woman.

Being under house arrest made it difficult to make a living, so Ngoyi poured her energy into writing letters to friends and activists around the world, as well as into her sewing.

"She loved sewing and making blouses for the ANC women's league," her adopted daughter, Memory Mphahlele recalled for a *Sunday Times Heritage* report.

"For 18 years this brilliant and beautiful woman spent her time in a tiny house, silenced, struggling to earn money by doing sewing," wrote her friend and ANC comrade Hilda Bernstein.

The unique memorial then, made by artist Stephen Maqashela, is a sculpture of a sewing machine ingenuously created from old car parts. Attached to the sewing machine needle is a sculpture of a blouse in green, black and yellow, the colours of the ANC.

THE CRADLE OF SOWETO

⑫

Traces of Mpanzaville

Open field behind Orlando stadium
Open: Guided visit with Tshenolo Mokhele
Tel: 084-715-3896

Take a walk through the open field alongside Klipspruit Valley Road (known locally as Killer Road) and peer closely at the ground. Among the long grass you will find the foundations of modern-day Soweto.

The Land Acts of 1913 and 1925 meant that black people were forbidden from owning land, but the simultaneous demands of the gold mining industry meant more and more labourers were required by the city of Johannesburg. By the 1940s, there was massive overcrowding in the black-designated township of Orlando.

It was into this charged atmosphere that Orlando horse trader and social activist James Mpanza founded the Sofasonke movement, spearheading a campaign of housing and shelter for all.

Mpanza had a chequered history. He had murdered an Indian man in a crime of passion and justice (the man had supposedly been abusing an African woman), served time in prison where he found God, and was later pardoned by the Duke of Kent.

Mpanza called himself "The Black Verwoerd" because, unlike the political leaders of the African National Congress, he believed firmly in separate development and that white people should build their own economy and leave the black man alone.

Perhaps the Julius Malema of his day, in March 1944, Mpanza led 200 women and children on a land grab, settling a shanty town on this piece of open tract next to Orlando. The illegal shanty town grew and grew, with 500 people arriving each day.

"It was an enclave which the system couldn't access. It had its own police force and its own way of supplying people with coal, bread and milk," says Tshenolo Mokhele, a distant relation who offers guided visits to Mpanza's home in Orlando.

Mpanzaville grew and grew, inspiring thirteen other settlements across the Witwatersrand, including Tembisa (meaning The Promise) on the East Rand.

"His bravery defied all odds. His land grabbing even inspired white squatters," says Mokhele.

In 1945, the government responded to the land grab by building proper suburbs to deal with the overcrowding — the birth of Soweto as we know it today.

Mokhele makes the point that the story of Mpanza was overshadowed in recent years by the headline-grabbing story of the ANC's liberation struggle.

"By not telling all the stories, we are robbing future generations of their own narratives, their own legacy. This is the cradle of Soweto: the all-conquering township of South Africa. Mpanza is the father of Soweto."

ORLANDO PIRATES PAINTING

A reminder of the pirate past

4503 Khunou Street
Orlando East

On the brick wall of 4503 Khunou Street is a Perspex-framed oil-on-metal painting of the first team to ever call themselves the Orlando Pirates.

The painting marks the original home and headquarters of the team's first president, Bethuel Mokgosinyana, who turned the boys from street players into professionals.

It all began in Soweto in 1937, a tough era when the streets were full of tsotsis.

A group of barefoot teenagers began playing soccer on an open patch of ground in Orlando East. Among their ranks were children of migrant workers who had moved to Johannesburg to work in the gold mines.

The young players were good — very good. A boxing instructor called Andries "Pele Pele" Mkhwanazi, who was also a soccer talent scout, encouraged the players to form a team. Mkhwanazi wanted to see the boys involved in something fun and constructive. They originally named themselves Orlando Boys Club, but by 1939, inspired by swashbuckling black and white film *The Sea Hawk* starring Errol Flynn, the team was renamed the Orlando Pirates.

Self-appointed social worker and keen footballer Bethuel Mokgosinyana, was impressed and invited the boys to play in his back yard.

Mokgosinyana was neither educated nor wealthy, but he was a skilled carpenter and built a room in his backyard in Orlando that later became the Pirates' clubhouse. Every Wednesday for 10 years, the boys gathered to discuss game strategy — Mokgosinyana always opened and closed these marathon sessions with a prayer — and on Fridays before matches the chosen team would camp out overnight, sleeping on the floor.

With his own money, Mokgosinyana bought the team their first kit and they adopted the skull and crossbones as their emblem. The Pirates first competed in the Johannesburg Bantu Association's Saturday League, winning the Division Two title, and by 1944 they were playing in Division One.

In the decades since, their success has taken them far away from those dusty streets of Soweto. In the 1970s they won four National Premier Soccer League titles; in 1995 they won the CAF Champions League; and in 1996 they won the African Super Cup, becoming the only South African team to do so. The Orlando Pirates' most recent appointee was Swedish coach Kjell Jonevret.

The painting, by artist Sam Nhlengethwa, a devout Orlando Pirates supporter since the age of five, is a reminder of how it all began.

BIRD WATCHING IN SOWETO

Looking for specials in Soweto

Klipspruit wetland
Soweto
Open: Daily
For bookings, contact Raymond Rampolokeng
Tel: 072-947-3311

The brightly painted cooling towers of the old Orlando power station have become an icon of Soweto. Most people know them for their popular bungee jump, but below the towers is an oasis of green surrounding a small lake, often overlooked even by Sowetans.

"When they think of greenery they think of the Kruger Park and the zoo," says Sowetan resident and ornithologist Raymond Rampolokeng, who works closely with Bird Life South Africa. "We're slowly introducing Sowetans to their own backyard."

During apartheid, this green belt was one of South Africa's first gated communities; this was where white government officials were billeted.

It was also where, as a child, Rampolokeng would come to hunt birds.

"There was a lack of private space in those small four-roomed houses, so we would go and play in the wetlands. We would make nets out of an old bike rim and a sack, and try catch birds to *braai* (grill) them," he says, shaking his head with a laugh as he remembers trying to catch Cape sparrow, laughing doves and house sparrows. "The only thing worth catching were striped rats. They were a delicacy. The birds just ended in burnt bones. We were naughty boys."

Nowadays, Rampolokeng takes visitors and local children into this wetland on picnics so they can discover the wildlife in their neighbourhood, and begin to understand the value it holds.

The wetland is a haven for Cape wagtails, Blacksmith lapwings, spur fowl, the Greater striped swallow (a migrant bird that visits each year from Asia and Europe) and orange-breasted waxbills. It also boasts one special, the squacco heron, along with African monarch butterflies.

"One of our biggest challenges is dumping. Most people are still concerned with bread and butter issues. We need to raise conservation issues among the residents. It's my lifelong dream of leaving a legacy where young people appreciate the area they are living in so they can hand the pride and resources over to a future generation."

At the moment, it's just a handful of old fishermen who treasure it. And a few kayakers.

"I come here to avoid my wife," jokes an old man, fishing for carp. "It's a place I come to find peace."

CREDO MUTWA VILLAGE

A magical cultural village

Oppenheimer Park
991 Bochabela St
Soweto
Open: Daily 6am—6pm

At the back of the Oppenheimer Park in Soweto, hand-painted onto a white notice board are these cautionary words:

Kwa-Khayalendaba, Home of the story. Enter in Peace. This place is no tourist attraction. It is a holy place where African cultures religions and indigenous sciences are recorded and preserved in pictures and sculpture form. Against the coming night, we shall preserve the light. All visitors are requested to give this place the same respect they would give to any place of religion.

All liars, fools, skeptics and atheists must please keep out. A curse lasting seven years shall fall to all who destroy any part of this place. They will be unlucky in all they do, be hunted like beasts, and finally die in agony in lonely places. BEWARE.

Enter and you find yourself in a magical cultural village, full of mesmerising sculptures and paintings all made by Credo Mutwa, the legendary Zulu historian, prophet, artist, shaman and writer. Mutwa penned the internationally acclaimed book *Indaba, My Children,* a collection of African folk tales published in 1964 that charts the story of African tribal life since the time of the Phoenicians.

Credo Mutwa was born in 1922 in Natal, the grandson of Ziko Shezi, a Bantu witch doctor who was the guardian of his tribe's history. In 1963, Mutwa himself was officially proclaimed High Witch Doctor, but the following year he broke his sacred tribal oath of secrecy by writing *Indaba, My Children*, which he wrote in response to the injustices against Africans and their culture.

The stories — beginning with the creation myth, when Ninavanhu-Ma, the Great Mother, created the human race — show how we all come from one branch. We may separate ourselves by saying that we are black, white, Indian, but the truth is that we are all connected.

Ivan Mothiba, a self-appointed guide who will show visitors around for a small donation, admits the place is not frequently visited. "It's more like a ghost this place, to most people. They think it's just a place of trees, they don't see what's in here."

A prophecy of two planes, flying into twin skyscrapers, painted in the 1970s

The cultural village is an experiential version of Credo Mutwa's book. It not only includes enormous sculptures of gods and mortals, myths and legends, but also some of Credo Mutwa's prophecies, including a painting of two planes, flying into twin skyscrapers ... painted in the 1970s.

ANTI-XENOPHOBIA SCULPTURES ⓰

Protest art in Diepkloof

Funda Community College
Zone 6 8642 Immink Drive (Opposite Lesedi Clinic)
Diepkloof
Soweto

A map of Africa created from shards of a broken mirror; a rocket-shaped man welded from chains, steel and woven grass; a steel woman with a torso like a tortoise shell, weighed down by the burdens of the continent.

Few will have seen these three sculptures, designed by artist and educator Charles Nkosi, built by his students, and tucked away in the studios of Funda, a community college in Diepkloof, Soweto.

The sculptures were not built for commercial ends, but as a way to process and reflect on the xenophobic attacks of 2009, when black South Africans turned on immigrants from the rest of the continent.

"It was our contribution towards black awareness against xenophobia; our contribution to the political crosswinds," says Nkosi. "Xenophobia affects all of us. When you hurt someone else, a lot of damage is done internally to the torturer."

Stand in front of the broken mirror of Africa and your reflection is returned to you, disturbed and distorted.

"It is a metaphoric representation of disfiguring," Nkosi explains. "You are disfiguring the image of Africa if you are doing that."

He points to the steel man bound in chains. "Chains can be used for slavery, but can also find the weakest link and the strongest link in a chain, so they also represent unity and unified movement."

The use of woven grass is about social cohesion.

Funda (Zulu for "to learn") is no stranger to creating art as protest. During the days of Bantu education, there were few places where young black artists could train. In the early 1980s, during the state of emergency, Funda became the place where black students with diminished artistic resources could develop their artistic consciousness, backed by private sector funding.

"An artist is a journalist in a way. Protesting was like trying to add to the voice of reason," says Nkosi.

Today, there are no restrictions on where and what black students can study, but Nkosi finds that kids from the most disadvantaged homes still struggle to find art as a solace. Which is where Funda comes in. With limited government funding and piecemeal private sector donations, it now runs part-time programmes for aspiring teenage artists, out-of-school youth and unemployed adults with a passion for art.

Nkosi says, "We help quench the thirst burning inside them."

ENOCH SONTONGA HILL

*A place of immense stillness,
where Nkosi Sikelel' iAfrika was written (perhaps)*

Soweto
Open: All day, every day

Up behind the University of Johannesburg's Soweto campus is Enoch Sontonga Hill, a craggy koppie where aloes and thorny acacia trees grow in abundance. It's the second highest spot in Soweto (after the cooling towers) and a place where you can get a 360-degree view of this enormous township, which, two decades after apartheid, is gradually morphing into a city in its own right.

The hill is named after Enoch Sontonga who composed *Nkosi Sikelel' iAfrika*, South Africa's national anthem, which for over a hundred years, was the liberation song of the African National Congress.

Sontonga had a short life: born in 1873 and educated in the eastern Cape, he became a teacher and choirmaster at a mission school in Nancefield — present day Klipspruit, Soweto. He died in 1905 at the age of 32.

Sontonga was deeply touched by the suffering of his fellow black South Africans during these early days of gold-mining fervour and would take frequent walks up into the hills, often with his exercise book under his arm, in which he would write the poetry that was later set to music to become songs of inspiration and strength for the oppressed during the last century.

There is no proof that Sontonga definitely wrote *Nkosi Sikelel' iAfrika* on this hill, but sitting up here on a rock, beside a prickly pear, listening to the sounds of Soweto — taxi horns, distant laughter and music — it is easy to imagine.

No matter how urban South Africa becomes, nature is always there, an indelible presence that seems to envelop and protect the nation. From this hill, Sontonga would have been able to see and hear the energy of a place in flux, while still connecting with an energy as old as time.

Today, as people fear crime, few choose to walk alone in Sontonga's footsteps. But if you do, you'll discover a place of immense stillness, that seems to float above the hustle and bustle of Soweto.

"Sitting up here you feel liberated," says Raymond Rampolokeng, a local environmentalist and ornithologist who brings people here for bird watching. "You feel the openness. With whatever is going on in South Africa, we need this."

SS MENDI MEMORIAL

To the memory of the men of the black Titanic

Avalon Cemetery
Tshabuse Street
Tshiawelo
Soweto
Open: Daily

Under the pine trees on the northern edge of the Avalon Cemetery, close to Tshiawelo train station, stands the memorial to the men of the *SS Mendi*, the troopship of the 5th Battalion South African Native Labour Corps (SANLC), which sank in the cold, foggy waters of the English Channel on 12 February 1917 while en route to France. The SANLC consisted of men who had been recruited throughout South Africa to serve not as armed soldiers, but as workers and labourers on war fronts.

The memorial was built in 1995 in time for the official state visit of Queen Elizabeth II. Inscribed on the memorial wall are the names of the 616 who drowned, as well as these words from Reverend Isaac Wauchope Dyobha, who served as a minister and interpreter with the SANLC, spoken as the ship went down.

"Be quiet and calm my countrymen, for what is taking place now is what you came here to do. We are all going to die, and that is what we came for. Brothers, we are drilling the death drill. I, a Zulu, say here and now that you are all my brothers... Xhosas, Swazis, Pondos, Basotho and all others, let us die like warriors. We are the sons of Africa. Raise your war cries my brothers, for though they made us leave our assegais back in the kraals, our voices are left with our bodies..."

The *SS Darro*, travelling at full speed and emitting no warning signals, had rammed the *SS Mendi*, sinking it in 20 minutes. The real horror of this tragedy is that no steps were taken by the *Darro* to lower boats or rescue the survivors. Rather, it stood off, and floated nearby while lifeboats from the *Mendi's* escorting destroyer, *HMS Brisk*, rowed among the survivors, trying to rescue them.

The sinking of the *SS Mendi* and the massive loss of life has passed into South African history as an epic tragedy that epitomises the grief and the losses of the First World War, specifically from the African perspective.

Local taxi driver Selloma Tshaba, who accompanied *Secret Johannesburg* to the site, remarked that he knew about the *Mendi*, but not the memorial.

"I nearly cried standing there. I didn't know so many had died," he said.

Avalon Cemetery is also the final resting place of legendary struggle icons, Hector Pietersen, Lilian Ngoyi, Joe Slovo and Helen Joseph.

THE SHARPEVILLE HUMAN RIGHTS PRECINCT

Sharpeville's tears

3847 Seeiso Street
Sharpeville Vereeniging

The Kwa-Dlomo Dam in Sharpeville, just outside of Vereeniging, used to be a piddly watering hole. It's said that the land owner, "Mr Dlomo", dug the hole so that he could lease grazing to township dwellers who weren't allowed to keep livestock at their homes.

It's hard to believe if you look at the dam now; the body of water extends to a width that is broad enough to host dinghies or paddle boats. The dam's consistent expansion is explained by the area's elders and is related to one of South Africa's most tragic political events — the Sharpeville Massacre of 21 March 1960.

"The *gogos* (grannies) say that after the massacre the rains came down, but only in the area where the bodies [had fallen]," says Petrus Maya from the Vaal Teknorama Museum, pointing to the borders of the memorial square and across the road to the former police station.

"The grandmothers believe that it was God washing away the tears and the blood and that it (the water and blood) flowed into the Dlomo Dam. The dam used to be small, only big enough for a few cattle, but after the massacre, the dam has grown bigger every year."

Now commemorated as Human Rights Day, the Sharpville Massacre was a turning point in history that garnered significant support against apartheid from the international community. The massacre was followed by an increase in protests across the country and ultimately led to a state of emergency. A total of 69 peaceful anti-passbook protestors died that day, many shot in the back by the security forces as they were running away.

The youngest victim was Bessie James, who was a mere 12 years old. Her short life is commemorated, along with the 68 other victims, by a series of white concrete pillars at the Sharpeville Human Rights Precinct, which stands as something of a white elephant in the dusty township.

A dozen or so teens hang out outside the precinct, thrusting their cellphones and tablets through the fencing in an attempt to pick the WiFi signal streaming from the main building. The patchy lawns around the pillars are maintained, but the water feature that once ran through it is dry. The precinct's exhibition centre houses a few battered photographs displayed on lopsided easels, and an old bicycle that was left behind after the massacre.

The gravesite of the victims at the Phelindaba Cemetery is in a similar state of neglect. Weeds crawl across the graves, which are adorned with dead bouquets. There is an additional memorial garden situated in the cemetery.

There might be more logical reasons than the gogos' stories to explain away the Dlomo Dam's expansion, perhaps due to the high water table in the area or human intervention, but in an age where history is so easily forgotten, it seems appropriate that the landscape should respond by swelling its waters to hold at least some of the tears from our past.

Greater Joburg: Alex and East

①	RASTA VILLAGE	180
②	IKASI GYM PAINTINGS	182
③	MOVING FEAST	184
④	WHERE GANDHI MEDITATED	186
⑤	THE LINKSFIELD HOME OF L. RON HUBBARD	188
⑥	SCHOENSTATT SHRINE	190
⑦	A SCENIC FLIGHT IN A DC3	192
⑧	GET MARRIED IN A BOEING 747	194
⑨	THE FLAMINGOS OF BENONI	196
⑩	SNOWBOARDING ON KLEINFONTEIN MINE DUMP	198
⑪	REDAN ROCK ENGRAVINGS	200
⑫	THE WHISKY TRAIN	202
⑬	COSMOS FLOWER PATHWAYS	204

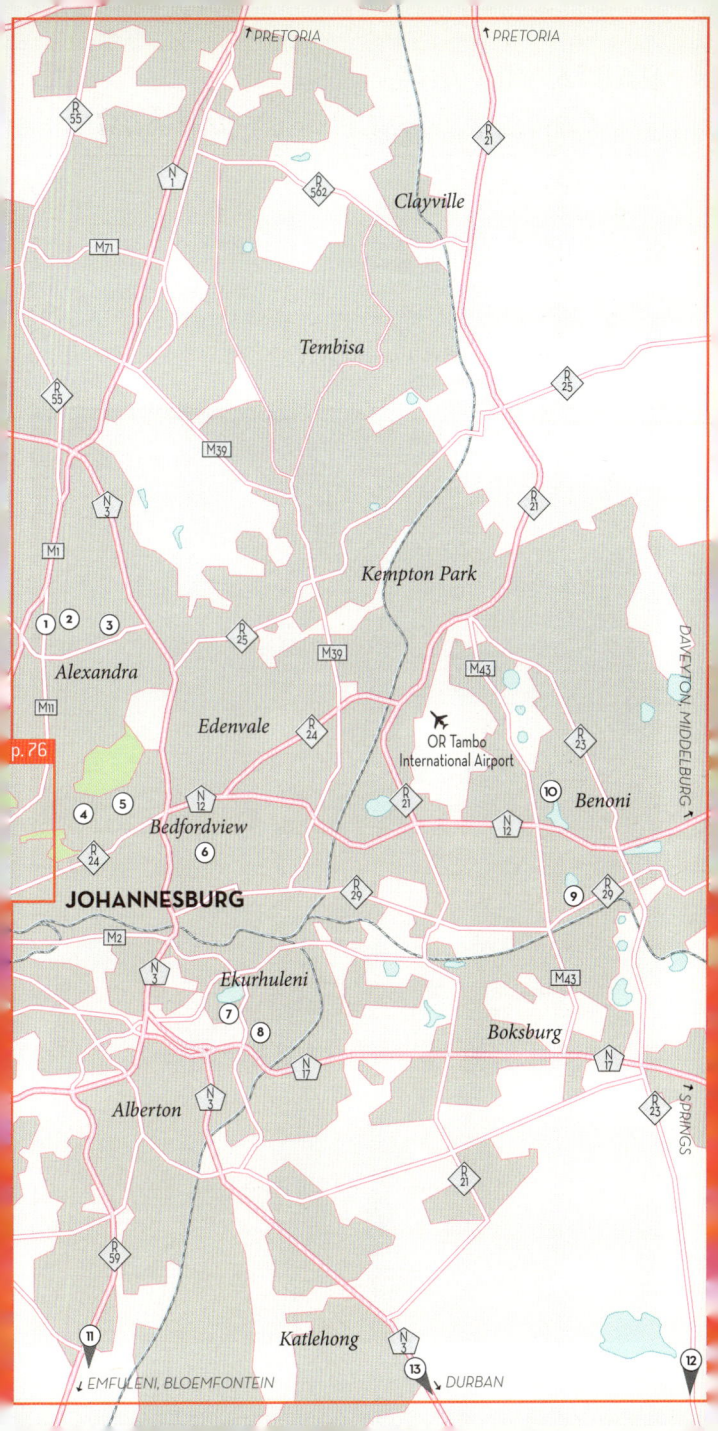

JOHANNESBURG

- Pretoria
- Clayville
- Tembisa
- Kempton Park
- Alexandra
- Edenvale
- OR Tambo International Airport
- Bedfordview
- Benoni
- Ekurhuleni
- Boksburg
- Alberton
- Katlehong
- Emfuleni, Bloemfontein
- Durban
- Springs
- Dayeton, Middelburg

p. 76

RASTA VILLAGE

A place of peace in Alex

Far Eastbank
Alexandra
Open for worship: Friday evening and all day on Saturday
Transport: Marlboro Gautrain station

On the banks of the Jukskei River, amid a sizeable plantation of marijuana, is Alexandra's Rasta village, the only dedicated Rasta community in Johannesburg.

There has been a Rasta community in Alex since the 1930s. During the height of apartheid, those fleeing the security police would hide in the river and find sanctuary with the Rastas.

The only other Rasta community in South Africa is Judah Square, residing in a small valley in Khayalethu South, a suburb of Knysna.

"I live up the road and I didn't even know this was here," says Asanda Daza, who makes a living as a guide, sharing the more well-known highlights of Alex with foreign tourists.

The village is a short walk from the Marlboro Gautrain station, and if you look out the window as the train nears the station, you can spot the red, green and gold flag flying in the near distance.

At the entrance is the brightly painted village spaza shop where peaceful souls are welcome to ask Rasta Torch — the elder of the Rastas — for permission to build small dwellings here.

"My job is to touch those who haven't got the mark of God. We are here to save their souls and put light into the people. We are peace in the community," says the dreadlocked Rasta Torch, who is hesitant to talk when we first arrive, but later joins us in the vast garden, dressed in a springbok skin and gladiator sandals.

Surrounded by burnt out candles and drums within a circular structure at the heart of the village are pictures of Haille Selassie, the regent of Ethiopia from 1913 to 1960, who the Rastafaris regard as the returned messiah of the Bible.

The Rasta time for worship is Friday evening and all day on Saturday.

"We chant, we pray and we meditate. Women, elders, youth, are all welcome," says Rasta Torch.

What makes the village particularly special is the large market garden, tended by Silas Chitengedza from northern Zimbabwe. He came to South Africa looking for work as a builder and instead found himself becoming a small-scale farmer.

Among his crops are tomatoes and spinach, which he sells for R5-R10 a bunch.

"I love this place because it is so peaceful. People come here to buy fresh vegetables from the garden," says Chitengedza, adding, "We don't sell marijuana."

IKASI GYM PAINTINGS

First Virgin Active in Alex

Richard Baloyi Street
Alexandra
Tel: 071-144-2252

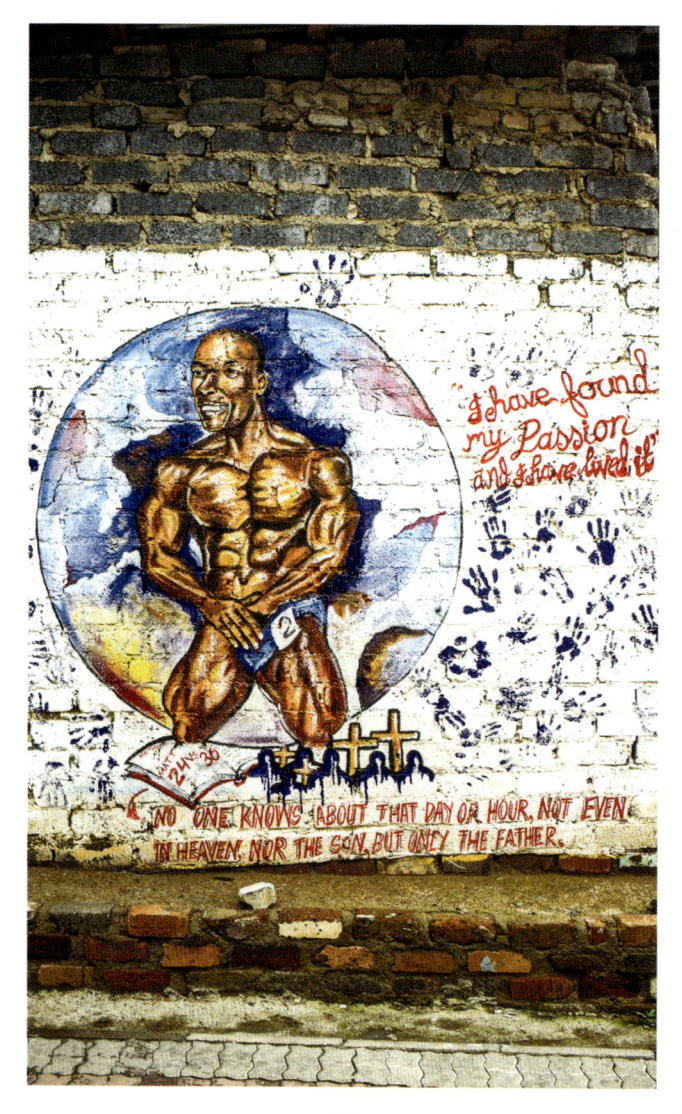

It all began with Tumi Tumelo Masite's mother. When Masite was a teenager, Alexandra was a tough place. Constant gang violence made the streets unsafe, so Mama encouraged him to clean up the yard and turn it into a makeshift gym. It was this dedicated space (and Masite's growing muscles) that caught the eye of Reg Park, personal trainer to Arnold Schwarzenegger.

Park was in Alex visiting the first home of Nelson Mandela (also on Richard Baloyi Street, marked by a blue plaque and a garden of murals). As a young man, Mandela had run away from the Eastern Cape and an arranged marriage, and arrived in Alex to seek his fortune, getting a first job as a night watchman at the Crown Mines. Samora Machel, the late president of Mozambique also lived briefly across the road from Mandela.

Park donated some dumbbells and federal barbells to Masite's garden gym, and arranged a meeting between Masite and the British entrepreneur, Richard Branson, who was in South Africa setting up the Virgin Active fitness chain.

Branson not only donated more equipment to the fledgling gym, he also invited Masite to train at the Virgin Active in Morningside, and funded him to study sports science, nutrition, and personal training.

His muscles, confidence and determination grew. In 2006, Masite competed in the Rainbow Classic body building championships, placing in the top three.

The walls of the gym are full of newspaper clippings that document the story of Masite's success, while the television cabinet of Mama's front room strains under the weight of his trophies.

Remarkably, like so many of Alex's residents, Masite is also an artist. Masite uses brightly coloured paints to channel township and jazz scenes. "You don't have to just look at my muscles and judge me," he says. "I am so much deeper inside."

While he is working on his next canvas, the iKasi gym is a treasured hub, not only for aspiring body builders, but also for recovering nyaope addicts, former prison inmates, and those trying to manage health conditions such as diabetes.

Masite believes, like many other young people, that the time has come to put Alex on the map.

"We want good things here, just like in Soweto," says Masite. "We want to create our own Vilakazi Street right here."

During the month of September, the many artists of Alex open up their homes, many of them small shacks, and exhibit their work.

MOVING FEAST ③

Fine dining in Alex

78 Starling Crescent
Eastbank
Alexandra
Open: Booking required
Tel: 082-864-6049

Five years ago, Happiness Makhalemele lived in a flat in a tough part of "Deep Alex", also often labelled by locals as "Gomorrah" or the "Dark City". Tired of working as a clerk at the traffic department, Happiness left her 9-to-5 job and started to follow her true passion: cooking.

She began by selling mince vetkoek at Alex's 15th street taxi rank. Her food was so popular, she sold out on a daily basis. Encouraged by her regular customers, she next began a pop-up restaurant in her small flat on Mondays, selling *mogudu* (tripe).

"People usually slaughter a cow on a Saturday, so on Monday you eat the innards," she explains.

"Mogudu Mondays" became so popular that Makhalemele raised enough capital to put a down payment on a home in Eastbank, on the more upmarket side of the Jukskei river. With the help of her husband and son, the latter of whom is a keen cook with plans to branch out on his own, they opened a daily restaurant in their home.

At first they served in the living room, but quickly outgrew the house. They now serve in a custom-built conservatory in the front garden.

"People in Alex love food," says Makhalemele. "With cooking we found an opportunity right here in Alex."

Alex sits awkwardly in many people's minds.

To many Joburgers, it is a considered a no-go zone, while at the same time it is a favourite hang-out destination of upwardly mobile black South Africans, who return from the suburbs to enjoy its buzz and unique vibe on weekends.

And while Makhalemele may have made her name initially from selling typically African dishes, her cuisine is much more extensive and inventive than the old favourites.

Her menu changes daily, and when *Secret Johannesburg* visited we ate a main course of large Mozambican prawns followed by an exquisite passion fruit cheesecake, each individually created inside a small glass while we were eating the main course.

To call Moving Feast fine dining is not to exaggerate. Each day Happiness Makhalemele creates a new menu and sends out her creation to a dedicated following of Alex foodies by Whatsapp.

Mondays, though, are still dedicated to Mogudu. Booking is essential.

WHERE GANDHI MEDITATED ④

A spiritual spot above the city

Harvey Nature Reserve
Linksfield Ridge

Mahatma Gandhi's Johannesburg life is well documented. He first came to South Africa in 1893 as a young lawyer and remained in the country for 21 years, preaching mass defiance and passive resistance to unjust laws, while advocating the rights of people across the racial and religious spectrum.

Over his years in Jo'burg, he lived at numerous addresses, including Tolstoy Farm in the south-west of Johannesburg (named after Russian novelist and philosopher Leon Tolstoy), where he and his followers lived out his philosophy of *satyagraha*, meaning "soul" or "truth force".

So powerful was the philosophy that the founders of the ANC adopted *satyagraha* in 1912. The first mass anti-apartheid programme, the Defiance Campaign of 1952, followed the pattern of passive resistance set by Gandhi.

Gandhi was also resident at 11 Albermarle Street in Troyeville (marked by a blue plaque), a four-roomed house in Bellevue East on the corner of Sharp and Albert Streets (now demolished).

One of his most famous homes, where he was thought to have developed his philosophy, was at 15 Pine Road, Orchards, on the northern slope of Linksfield Ridge. The house was designed by his close friend architect Hermann Kallenbach to resemble a traditional African farm, or *kraal*. Kallenbach and Gandhi lived here together from 1908 to 1909. Today it is a little-known B&B and meditation retreat called Satyagraha House, but what is even less known is that Gandhi would walk and meditate daily up on the ridge.

As a child, San Francisco-based architect Allan Schwartz remembers Kallenbach pointing out the meditation sites to him. As a youth, Schwartz was dreaming of becoming an architect and would sometimes spend whole days with Kallenbach, who was a family friend.

"Kallenback said Gandhi would sit on the southern side of the ridge, facing towards Kensington," says Schwartz.

Today the area is more populated than it would have been during Gandhi's times, but it is still possible to find a peaceful, unchanged corner in the Harvey Nature Reserve on the western end of this four kilometre ridge. Donated to the city in 1959 by Sydney Harvey, the north facing slopes are dense with trees and shrubs, while those facing south are abundant with grasslands, aloes and proteas. During the summer months, orchids bloom and other wild flowers thrive after the winter veld fires. Look closely and you can also spot late Iron Age Tswana sites, some small wildlife, and of course, the spirit of Gandhi.

THE LINKSFIELD HOME OF L. RON HUBBARD

Ron the Zulu

40 Hannaben Street
Cyrildene
Open: Seven days a week
Free entry
Tel: 0110-540-540
Email: Tours@LRonHubbard.org.za

Entering the modernist Johannesburg home of controversial Scientology founder L. Ron Hubbard has the feel of entering a 1960s soap opera, featuring the hip, established and well-to-do. The house was designed in 1951/52 by architect Frank L. Jarret for a timber merchant, which explains the extensive use of fine wood in the flooring, wall paneling and cabinets throughout the home. The floors and doors are teak, the thresholds are Japanese oak and the panels are Oregon pine.

Perched on the Linksfield ridge, the house boasts enviable views over the suburbs and city, particularly at night when the surrounding buildings are lit up. "Sometimes I come in here at night and think I've left the lights on in the house, it's so bright," says Puneet Dhamija, who takes care of the house.

From the old dial up phone, 1960s furnishing to the light fittings and décor, it's a time capsule so perfectly preserved that if L. Ron himself were to be beamed down through the circular skylights in the entrance it would barely seem amiss.

Hubbard lived in the house from September 1960 to March 1961, a relatively short period in which he appears to have achieved a considerable amount. This includes, according to the LRH website, authoring, "a 'one man, one vote' constitution for apartheid-shackled South Africa. He likewise presented a Bill of Rights and penal code for equality and justice." You can find framed copies of these in the front room of house.

While it's doubtful that his writings had any bearing on the Convention for a Democratic South Africa (Codesa) and the final legislation that led South Africa to democracy in 1994, Hubbard certainly notched up a great number of plaques and accolades from the grateful recipients of his teachings.

Among these is a leather shield presented by The National Traditional Healers Association bearing possibly the highest honour that can be bestowed, a Zulu name: Mbuzeni — which means 'Ask me how I channel the way'.

The house is one of six perfectly restored and preserved homes (the other five being in the United States and England) that represent every residence of importance from 1950 to 1965 in terms of the founding and growth of Scientology.

SCHOENSTATT SHRINE

The free-thinking rebel's chapel

Corner of Florence Avenue and Van Buuren Road Bedford view
Open: 7am—6pm every day

Behind a hedge of jasmine, not far from Eastgate shopping centre, is a sanctuary of calm. You feel it the moment you step out of the car and walk towards the tiny white chapel set in the corner of verdant gardens, watched over by giant trees.

The little-known shrine is part of the Schoenstatt Apostolic Movement, founded by Father Joseph Kentenich in Germany in 1914. As a young priest, concerned about regimental thinking within the church and society and with how the conflicting, idealistic doctrines of Communism, National Socialism and Capitalism were being billed as *the* solutions to the world's problems, Kentenich established a new movement with a handful of young seminarians to combat mechanistic thinking.

Kentenich believed that through a deeper contemplation of Mary, a strong-willed woman, with an independent mind, yet still guided by her faith, people could begin to forge their own, authentic Christian voice, rather than just be theological puppets.

He obtained permission to use an abandoned garden shed, formerly a cemetery chapel, and turned it into a place for retreat, prayer and pilgrimage, where people could find deeper self-knowledge and inner freedom.

Unsurprisingly his belief in the free-thinking individual didn't sit well with the Nazis: during the Second World War, Kentenich was imprisoned at Dachau concentration camp, along with 2600 other priests, for speaking out against Nazi ideology. It was during his internment there that he established a global vision for spreading what he called the 'Covenant of Love'. In 1948, he established shrines in Brazil, Chile, Argentina, Uruguay, the United States and South Africa. The shrine in Bedfordview is the only one in the world to be built by its members. Like all Schoenstatt shrines, it is a replica of the original chapel in Germany.

That's not to say the road was smooth. In 1949, a treatise Kentenich wrote on the dangers of mechanistic thinking and living, even within the Catholic Church, brought him into confrontation with Church circles. From 1951—1965, the church exiled him to Milwaukee in the USA and he was removed from his young movement. Only in 1965 was he exonerated by papal decree and returned to the Schoenstatt Movement in Germany.

In South Africa, where patriarchy still sits heavy on the nation, fuelling deplorable levels of rape and domestic abuse, this unique chapel that pays homage to the female energy and independent spirit of Mary is indeed a unique beacon of light.

A SCENIC FLIGHT IN A DC3

⑦

Still taking to the skies more than 70 years after serving with Allied forces in Egypt in WWII

Skyclass Aviation
Rand Airport
Germiston
Open: Once a month by appointment
Tel: 011-541-9911

They don't make them like this any more. The gleaming silver flying machine parked on a private airfield is the stuff that dreams are made of. The Douglas DC3 Dakota "Klapperkop" not only looks good, she is still taking to the skies more than 70 years after being built in Oklahoma City and serving with Allied forces in Egypt in World War Two.

This was the legendary plane that made air travel popular — a piece of aviation history that flew in D-Day and featured in the last scene of *Casablanca*. Painted to represent the DC3s that began service with South African Airways during the 1940s, the plane's main task nowadays is to take passengers, once a month, on low-level nostalgia trips across the Jo'burg skyline, taking off from Rand Airport in Germiston.

On a cloudless and windless day, the plane takes 28 passengers on a 20-minute scenic flight towards Soccer City in Soweto, banking north to fly over the Mall of Africa in Midrand, and back to Rand Airport via Sandton City and Ellis Park Stadium (R850pp). However, trips on the 'vomit comet' (the less romantic name for this non-pressurised bird) will be cancelled if weather conditions are too adverse.

Once back on land, Paul Roberts, the airport's security manager offers free tours, by appointment, of the airport hangars, home to over 300 privately owned aircraft, many of them classics. Among the beauties are DC4s, DC6s and some Harvards, the two-seater with the raspy engine that the South African air force used up until 1994 to train fighter pilots. The Harvards are preserved as national heritage items by the Heritage Council of South Africa.

It is also possible to arrange for scenic flights out of the Swartkop base outside Pretoria in a Harvard plane.

Art Deco at the airport

Rand airport itself is worthy of a visit. Johannesburg's main airport until the 1950s, the art deco terminal building, complete with an avenue of palm trees, has stood in for Miami and Burbank airports in Hollywood films, and also starred in the Amelia Earhart Story with A-list actors Hilary Swank and Richard Gere. It also has a pretty decent bar and restaurant, where you can while away an afternoon, listening to live music, drinking beer, eating pizza and watching the planes take off and land.

GET MARRIED IN A BOEING 747 ⑧

On a wing and a prayer

South African Airways Museum Society
Old Transvaal Aviation Club building
Dakota Crescent
Rand Airport
Germiston
Open: Daily, except Mondays
Tel: 076-879-5044

Few South Africans will forget that moment on 24 June 1995, when the Boeing 747 *Lembombo* roared over Ellis Park stadium at the start of the match in which South Africa beat New Zealand to claim the Rugby World Cup. It was the team's first world cup after being readmitted to global competition with the end of apartheid. The world had collective goosebumps at the end of the match when Nelson Mandela, wearing the number six Springboks rugby shirt — the same shirt worn by team captain Francois Pienaar — presented the Rugby World Cup trophy to Pienaar.

Lebombo was retired in 2004, but did not end up on a scrap heap. For her last flight, the 30-year-old dame took 291 passengers, including the technical crew that had looked after her, on a short flight over Hartebeespoort dam.

"It's like losing a friend," Captain Denis Spence told *The Star* on the day of the aircraft's retirement. "But at the same time, it is history in the making. Life goes on and we need to make way for new technology and new planes."

Lebombo then settled into her new life as a museum piece and a wedding venue.

Retired Captain Samuel Rautenbach — who first flew *Lebombo* home in 1973 from Seattle (where she was built) via London (where her seats were fitted), "She was a beaut to fly!" — now volunteers as a weekend guide at the museum and can be hired as a celebrant. Couples can choose between getting married standing in one of the engines, or in the first class cabin, in which Rautenbach once flew Frank Sinatra and his wife, who were travelling from New York to Johannesburg for the opening of Sun City. On that occasion, Sun International chartered the whole plane and turned the upstairs into a bedroom for Sinatra.

Parked alongside *Lebombo* on the tarmac at the South African Aviation Museum is another smaller 747, also available for nuptials. *Maluti* was custom built for South African Airways during apartheid. The plane was able to fly extra fast and extra high in order to avoid detection during the days when South African aircraft were banned from flying over African airspace.

Perfect for shotgun brides.

There are also two reception spaces at the museum, and another restaurant with runway views at the nearby Rand Airport. Perfect for a quick honeymoon escape.

THE FLAMINGOS OF BENONI

A quiet idyll, home to 110 species of birds

Korsman's Bird Sanctuary
The Drive
Lakefield

"I used to drive hundreds of kilometres to Kruger National Park to find a place to indulge in obsessive birdwatching. Then one blessed day, out of the blue, there was Korsman's," says amateur wildlife photographer Jan de Beer, who took the pictures featured here.

It is not surprising that de Beer, a long-time resident of the East Rand, had never heard of this fenced-in pan. Benoni has long been the butt of many South African jokes. Even the fact that its most famous export is the Hollywood star Charlize Theron has not been able to rescue this East Rand town from being billed as the capital of nowhere.

This is perhaps precisely why the birds like it. Tucked away in a boomed residential area, this fenced-in pan, with a circumference of 2.5 kilometres, is a quiet idyll that, across different months of the year, is home to 110 species of birds.

The fabulous pink flamingos might provoke the most surprise, but there are also Egyptian Geese, Goliath Herons, Sacred Ibis, Black Australian Swans, African Darters, kingfishers, the list goes on. According to de Beer, observing the pan brings constant surprises for the birdwatcher. One day he noted the unexpected arrival of a few small Marsh Sandpipers — who normally frequent Eastern Europe and central Asia — while at other times he clocks the Little Stints who stop in after their marathon flights from the North Pole.

And it's not just the birds that find respite here. At last count, there were 35 species of butterflies. And often spotted chilling out on a log just above the surface of the water — a terrapin.

As is typical of a bird sanctuary, humans are kept out (a green fence surrounds the pan), but volunteers have built four mounds outside the fence, with benches on top, so it is possible to relax up high and look down on a flurry of feathery comings and goings without getting too close and causing unwanted disruptions. That said, photographers who do want to be closer may volunteer to join one of the weekend work parties and help remove invasive vegetation in exchange for some tripod time.

"It is not only a place for wonderful photography, but also a place to find solace among the birds and lift the spirit," says de Beer.

SNOWBOARDING ON KLEINFONTEIN MINE DUMP

⑩

A golden opportunity for adventure

Snake Road offramp from the N1
Benoni
www.purerush.co.za

There is no symbol for Johannesburg quite as pervasive as the mine dump. Historically, they form the backbone of the city; the monolithic slabs of compacted dirt have come to assume almost as many meanings as there are people affected by them. For some they stand for labour and oppression, for others wealth and power. The politics and economy surrounding them has certainly served to highlight the discrepancies between rich and poor.

There are even individuals who see them as a place for religious contemplation or artistic inspiration. William Kentridge, South Africa's most well-known international artist, uses the mine dumps as a metaphor for the layering of memory as well as a terrain for nostalgia and loss.

And then, of course, there are those who see the mine dumps as nothing more than a giant playground. Head to the Kleinfontein Mine Dump — known as Benoni's Mountain by locals, or Mount Mayhem by adventurers — on any given weekend to find scores of adrenaline junkies navigating the slopes in 4x4s, on scramblers, mountain bikes or, most popularly, snowboards.

Although the same boards are used, it's not quite the same as snowboarding. For one, you don't zigzag down the slope to control your speed as you would with snow. Instead, you need to lean your weight backwards to propel yourself down the slope face forward.

The fine particles created during gold extraction create a powdery surface that isn't quite as slick as snow, but still allows boarders to hit speeds higher than they might on beach or desert sand dunes.

The sport was pioneered in Johannesburg by Pure Rush Industries, an adventure sports company that has set up ramps on Mount Mayhem. The company holds sandboarding lessons and rents boards to anyone keen to try out this golden opportunity for speed.

That said, aspiring sandboarding champs will have to find another man-made mountain to practice from in the next few years. The Kleinfontein Mine Dump, like many others surrounding the city, is slowly disappearing from Johannesburg's skyline as it is re-mined for the estimated 3.5 tons of gold it still contains. Modern extraction methods are far superior to those used in the pioneering days and most of the dumps are still valuable resources for the precious metal.

REDAN ROCK ENGRAVINGS

Song of the ancestors

1 Beethoven Street
Duncanville
Vereeniging
Open: To view the site and arrange a guide, contact the Vaal Teknorama Museum
Tel: 016-450-3030/1/2

There is a rumour that if you sit quietly on a certain sandstone outcrop nestled in the long grass in Redan outside of Vereeniging, at the time when the sky is turning to shades of pink and burnt umber, you'll hear the ancestors singing.

"I've had that experience myself. I've heard drums and something like stamping feet, but you never see anything," says Petrus Maya from the Vaal Teknorama Museum. "I was so shocked, I thought, 'Where are these people who are singing?' I thought maybe it was ghosts, but then other people told me, 'No, it is the ancestors'."

Regardless of whether you hear them, you will find evidence of our forebears on the Redan rocks near Vereening. Over 240 petroglyphs constitute the only major rock engraving site in Gauteng and are evidence of what was once a rich landscape brimming with fossil plants and Stone Age tools and remnants.

It's a little tricky to see them at first, but once you've spotted your first engraving, they seem to pop up everywhere, like mushrooms. No two images are the same, although the majority comprises abstract circular designs that were initially believed to depict the sun and belong to a "solar cult". This idea was later dismissed when archaeologists realised that some of the so-called "rays" were confined to the circumference of the circles.

There are also some obviously representational carvings, including a very clear image of a feline, an antelope and a rectangular shape topped with a circle that is believed to be the image of a person.

Despite having been declared a national monument, the site is neglected and in danger of decimation. For one, there is no barrier or fencing protecting the rocks from humans or cattle traipsing over them. And there is at least one incident of graffiti — some lewd words painted on the rocks in correction fluid, possibly by one of the learners at the nearby high school.

More concerning is the high level of air pollution. The Redan site falls into part of an industrial hotspot comprising Vanderbijlpark, Vereeniging and Sasolburg, and the corrosive air pollutants are gradually eroding the friable sandstone on which the engravings are etched.

I don't know if these are going to be around in 10 to 15 years time," says Maya. "I doubt it."

THE WHISKY TRAIN

A momentary truce

Val Hotel
Val
Tel: 082-550-5540
Email: info@valhotel.co.za
www.valhotel.co.za

The scars of the animosity between Boer and Brit over the First and Second Anglo Boer Wars — fought from 1880 to 1881 and 1899 to 1902 respectively — can be found across the South African landscape. So it's refreshing to find evidence of a momentary truce and some festive cheer between the warring sides.

In December 1900, Boer brothers Jack and Gert van den Heever found themselves slinking through the long grass alongside a railway line not far from the hamlet of Val, about 150 kilometres from Johannesburg. The tracks, which ran from Volksrust to Germiston (formerly Elandsfontein), had become a British lifeline for the supply of ammunition and food after they captured Johannesburg and Pretoria.

The brothers aimed to blow up the train and would have hidden in one of the many undulations in the ground for a number of hours close to the culvert where the explosives were hidden. Their persistence paid off more handsomely than expected. The train's trucks that were overturned spilled out a precious cargo of champagne, whisky and fine food, intended for the British officers' Christmas and New Year parties in the city.

For the half-starved troops on both sides it must have seemed like a glorious bonanza. The men tucked in with vigor, drowning their sorrows and forgetting, at least for a short while, the horror and inhumanity of war as well as the need to call another human, "enemy". Apparently, five ox wagons were later loaded with the excess booze and carted away by the Boers.

In 2012, with help from an anonymous donor, Rita Britz, who owns the Val hotel with her husband Andre, spearheaded a campaign to have a plaque erected to commemorate the event. The hotel is a wonderful place to raise some cheer and to learn all there is to know about the history of the surrounding area dating back to the Stone Age — Britz is an incredibly knowledgeable source.

Situated about four kilometres from the culvert, the hamlet of Val was initially established as a stagecoach route, and later a railway station. It didn't grow much over the years and still only comprises the hotel, a police station, a small church, four houses, a small graveyard and 28 inhabitants. There's a small informal museum attached to the hotel where, among old photos and other memorabilia, you can view the town's old telephone exchange.

COSMOS FLOWER PATHWAYS
⑬

Blooms of war

Heidelberg — take the R23 off-ramp from the N3 highway about 50 km from Johannesburg
Die Bakoond — corner of HF Verwoerd & Fenter Streets, Heidelberg
Kloof Cemetary, Fenter Street, Heidelberg

Every autumn, the countryside surrounding Johannesburg comes alive with rambling sprays of pink, white and mauve flowers. Cosmos (*Cosmos bippinatus*) is such an ingrained part of the seasonal cycle that it may come as a surprise that these cheerful blooms are, in fact, foreign immigrants.

The careful observer will note that the flowers choose to grow along particular roadsides, usually in peri-urban regions or farmland outside of the city, and it is precisely this growth pattern that offers a clue to their origin. The pathways now marked with exuberant blooms mirror those carved by British troops traipsing the countryside with their horses and oxen to carry the infrastructure of war to the Boers.

During the winter months when fodder was scarce, the British would import hay from Argentina, mixed into which would be cosmos seeds inadvertently imported from their country of origin. As a result, you still find thickets of the flowers everywhere the British and their animals went.

It's no surprise then that you'll find an abundance of the blooms around the region of Heidelberg, about 50 kilometres from Johannesburg. This town was an important centre in both of the wars.

During the First Anglo-Boer War (1880 to 1881) the town served as a capital of the Zuid Afrikaanse Republiek, an independent Boer state. To protect the town's water source from poisoning by their enemy, the Boers erected a *bakoond* (baking oven) — a long, rectangular, dome-like structure resembling a wood-fuelled oven — over their fresh water spring to disguise it.

The British gained control of the town during the Second Anglo-Boer War (1899 to 1902) and went about implementing a "scorched earth" policy — looting and burning Boer farms. Any women and children, servants or men who were unable to fight were sent to concentration camps.

Although the Heidelberg camps were considered to be "well run" and never exceeded 1,200 people, the conditions were still less than desirable and 624 white people died while interned there. In the nearby African concentration camp, 400 people died. The graves of the deceased can still be found in the Kloof and concentration camp cemeteries.

ALPHABETICAL INDEX

A collection of 16th, 17th and 18th century harpsichords	24
A scenic flight in a DC3	192
Adolf Hitler's typewriter	68
Anglo American doors	30
Anti-xenophobia sculptures	170
Baldinelli's mosaic of Jesus	78
Bambanani Urban Garden	94
Bird watching in Soweto	166
Byzantine plumber's yard	104
Cecily Sash mosaic in Little Ethiopia	46
Champion Trees	124
Church of St. Nicholas of Japan	126
Corner House's cupola	42
Cosmos flower pathways	204
Credo Mutwa village	168
Cuthbert's cupola	44
David Webster House	102
Diaz Cross	20
Edoardo Villa's "Confrontation" sculpture	144
Edoardo's villa	140
Enoch Sontonga Hill	172
Fietas Museum	122
Garden of St. Christopher	142
Gauteng's artesian spring	132
Get Married in a Boeing 747	194
Herman Charles Bosman in Johannesburg	92
Highlands Road Scottish vestiges	100
Historic French press in "The Atelier"	118
Houghton waterfall	82
Hyde Park shopping centre art collection	114
iKasi gym paintings	182
Iron Age furnaces buried in a park	148
JFK Memorial	150
Kerk Street Mosque	26
Lam Rim Tibetan Buddhist Centre	120
Larry Scully murals	52

Lilian Ngoyi memorial	160
Lindfield Victorian House Museum	128
Luscious lips graffiti	16
Magnetic rocks of Obs	86
Mandela's missing pistol	146
Masterpieces in the Magistrate's Court	32
Melville waterfall	116
Miniature railway of Observatory	84
Mogale's Gate Biodiversity Centre	154
Mother Theresa's blessing	58
Moving Feast	184
Mr. Trilety's nose shaper	106
MTN art collection	158
Nameless graves of the Burgershoop Cemetery	156
Old Johannesburg Stock Exchange trading floor	28
Old Protest Treasures	22
Orlando Pirates painting	164
Poetry steps	56
Post office murals	66
Rasta village	180
Redan rock engravings	200
Robert "Spiller" van Tonder grave	152
Rock art of the Volk	36
Rockface	40
Salisbury House	72
Schoenstatt Shrine	190
Sculptures in an overgrown lot	98
Snowboarding on Kleinfontein Mine Dump	198
Sons of England cross	80
Sophiatown's heritage tree	136
SS Mendi Memorial	174
St. Mary's the Less church	70
The Bernberg dresses	18
The cradle of Soweto	162
The Flamingos of Benoni	196
The Green Office	64

ALPHABETICAL INDEX

The lighthouse in the sky	38
The Linksfield home of L. Ron Hubbard	188
The Messerschmitt 262 jet night fighter	112
The old Victorian Hothouse	60
The paranoid tree	130
The Sharpeville Human Rights Precinct	176
The spaceship mast	48
The springbok of the regimental HQ of the Transvaal Scottish	108
The Strange stacks	34
The street art of Hannelie Coetzee	14
The Whisky Train	202
Transnet's mystery archive	50
Trevor Huddleston's cenotaph	134
Troyeville's "Bedtime Story"	96
Twist Street Bench	62
Vestiges of a tram station	74
Villa Arcadia	110
Where Gandhi meditated	186
Windybrow	54
Yeoville's festival bells	90
Yukon's missing windows	88

NOTES

NOTES

NOTES

NOTES

NOTES

NOTES

NOTES

ACKNOWLEDGEMENTS:

Our thanks to the people of Jo'burg, her guardians and champions, especially Flo Bird and Sarah Welham from the Johannesburg Heritage Foundation, Andrew Lindsay, James Ball, Brian McKechnie, Asanda Daza, Harry Nakeng, Raymond Rampolokeng, Karel Nel, Menzi Mbonambi, Johan Bruwer, Rodney Kruger, William Martinson, Christine McDonald, Sandile Radebe, Lucille Davie, Niel Nortje, Yolanda Meyer, Wendy Carstens, Helen and Darryl Torr, Allan Sinclair, Sandi MacKenzie, Alkis Doucakis, Jane Trembath, Jan de Beer and Robin Fee.

Photography credits::
Photos by C. L. Bell and Lisa Johnston.
Mandela's missing pistol, courtesy of Liliesleaf.
Flamingos of Benoni, picture by Jan De Beer.
MTN art collection, picture by Yinka Shonibare.

Maps: Cyrille Suss - Layout design: Coralie Cintrat - Layout: Alessio Melandri
Proofreading: Matt Gay - Edition: Stephanie Jonglez and Eleni Salemi

In accordance with jurisprudence (Toulouse 14-01-1887), the publisher is not to be held responsible for any involuntary errors or omissions that may appear in the guide despite the care taken by the editorial staff.
Any reproduction of this book in any format is prohibited without the express agreement of the publisher.

© JONGLEZ 2018
Registration of copyright: April 2018 – Edition: 01
ISBN: 978-2-36195-220-4
Printed in Bulgaria by Dedrax